BLAZING SADDLES

MEETS

YOUNG

FRANKENSTEIN

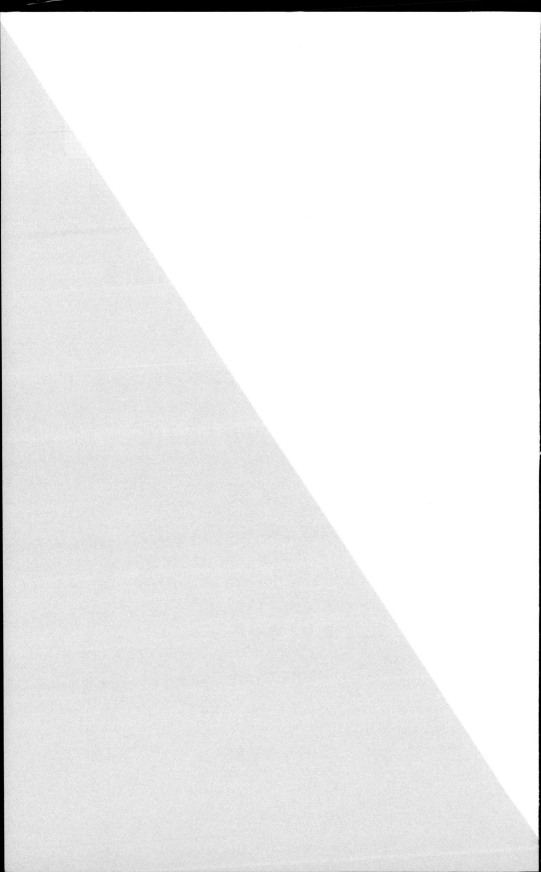

BLAZING SADDLES
MEETS
YOUNG
FRANKENSTEIN

The 50th Anniversary
of the Year of Mel Brooks

Bruce G. Hallenbeck

APPLAUSE
THEATRE & CINEMA BOOKS

Bloomsbury Publishing Group, Inc.
4501 Forbes Blvd., Ste. 200
Lanham, MD 20706
ApplauseBooks.com

Distributed by NATIONAL BOOK NETWORK

Library of Congress Cataloging-in-Publication Data

Names: Hallenbeck, Bruce G., 1952- author.
Title: Blazing saddles meets Young Frankenstein : the 50th anniversary of
   the year of Mel Brooks / Bruce G. Hallenbeck.
Description: Essex, Connecticut : Applause, [2025] | Includes
   bibliographical references and index.
Identifiers: LCCN 2024010405 (print) | LCCN 2024010406 (ebook) | ISBN
   9781493078004 (paperback) | ISBN 9781493078011 (epub)
Subjects: LCSH: Blazing saddles (Motion picture) | Young Frankenstein
   (Motion picture) | Comedy films—United States—History and criticism |
   Motion pictures—Production and direction—United States—History—20th
   century. | Brooks, Mel, 1926—-Criticism and interpretation. | Motion
   picture producers and directors—United States—Biography. | Nineteen
   seventy-four, A.D.
Classification: LCC PN1997.B67137 H35 2025 (print) | LCC PN1997.B67137
   (ebook) | DDC 791.43/61709730904—dc23/eng/20240611
LC record available at https://lccn.loc.gov/2024010405
LC ebook record available at https://lccn.loc.gov/2024010406

To Mel Brooks, Gene Wilder, and, as always, to my wonderful wife Rosa

Contents

CONTENTS

Acknowledgments

I couldn't have written this book without the help of the following people: my fearless agent Lee Sobel; my peerless editor John Cerullo; and
a special thanks to screenwriter and film scholar Dr. Steve Haberman,
coauthor of *Love Stinks* and *Dracula: Dead and Loving It* for granting
me a lengthy interview and filling me in with countless details about
Mel Brooks and his work.

Introduction: 1974

They don't make years like 1974 anymore. Pop culture was exploring themes that had never been allowed to be depicted before, thanks to the relaxed censorship of the times. Television shows such as *All in the Family* pushed the boundaries of what sitcoms—and the medium itself—could be. Made-for-television movies such as *The Autobiography of Miss Jane Pitman* proved that television could be just as socially relevant as theatrical films, and another TV movie, *Born Innocent*, starring Linda Blair of *The Exorcist* fame, proved that television could be just as shocking as theatrical films in its depiction of a gang rape (by other girls) of Blair's character, in which the rapists used a plunger handle. It was a time of controversial, thought-provoking and envelope-pushing subject matter in every medium, and *Born Innocent* became the highest-rated TV movie of the year.

Perhaps to counter this trend, Billboard's top two songs of the year were the schmaltzy *The Way We Were*, warbled by Barbra Streisand (from the hit movie of the same name) and the even schmaltzier *Seasons in the Sun* by Terry Jack. The biggest pop star of the year, though, was probably Elton John, whose album *Goodbye Yellow Brick Road* became something of a cultural phenomenon.

In the fashion world, leisure suits were introduced, and elegance took a nose dive. In literature, the first book by an author named Stephen King was published. It was called *Carrie*, and it made King—who wrote the book when he was living in a trailer—into an overnight success. Another book, *All the President's Men* by Carl Bernstein and Bob Woodward, reflected the year's largest scandal, Watergate, which culminated in the resignation of president Richard M. Nixon on August 8, 1974.

My personal fondness for that year is perhaps better understood when you consider the fact that it was the year I lost my virginity (in the back seat of a Chevy, no less) with my first love. There was another rite of passage that year, though, not just for me, but for a lot of other people my age: going to see a little film called *Blazing Saddles*, directed by Mel Brooks. Released on February 7 of that year, Brooks's uproarious parody became an instant cultural touchstone.

Blazing Saddles could not have been made even a few years previously, as censorship of the time would not have allowed it. After the creation of the American movie rating system in 1968, subjects that would have been taboo a few years earlier were finally allowed to be portrayed on-screen. *Blazing Saddles* tackled racism and prostitution, among other topics, but most of all it was a parody of classic Hollywood westerns produced in R-rated form that caused audiences of the time to laugh uproariously in spite of (or because of) its "politically incorrect" and sometimes downright offensive jokes. As times have changed again since 1974, it probably wouldn't be produced today.

Later in 1974, and just in time for Christmas, Brooks's *Young Frankenstein* was released. Another triumph for the filmmaker, both critically and commercially, *Young Frankenstein* quickly became another neo-classic, filmed in glorious black and white to recreate the look of the old Universal Pictures horror films, of which it was an affectionate parody. While not as groundbreaking as *Blazing Saddles* (which, among other things, broke the cinematic "fart barrier"), it continued in the tradition of Brooks's previous film in that it changed the face of movie parodies—and of horror films as well, as it turned out. *Young Frankenstein* was the second in a comedic one-two punch from Brooks in less than a year, a rarity in motion picture history for any director.

This book will attempt to put these two beloved classics into historical perspective in the context of an era when breaking down barriers and societal taboos was becoming the norm in pop culture. The journey from *All in the Family*, which made fun of racists, to *Blazing Saddles* (which did the same) was not much of a trek. Similarly, *Andy Warhol's Frankenstein* (a.k.a. *Flesh for Frankenstein*), released a few months earlier than *Young Frankenstein*, paved the way for Brooks's more refined take on the same subject. There were many more influences in between, however, many of them forgotten today, while Brooks's two classic parodies are still being talked about in the twenty-first century—and are widely regarded as his two best films.

One thing is for certain: *Blazing Saddles* could only have been made in the free-wheeling, anything-goes decade of the 1970s, an era when hard-core porn could be shown in a mainstream theater and political correctness was years in the future. *Young Frankenstein*'s slightly gentler humor is still very much of its time and, while a similar film *could* be made today, the fact is, it's a spoof that has never been bettered.

Let's return, then, to that madcap year when hair was long on boys and girls, bell bottoms were still popular, Nixon was out and Gerald Ford was in, and Mel Brooks and his laugh machine reigned supreme at the venue that was just beginning to blossom—the multiplex.

Bruce G. Hallenbeck

January 2024

Part I

BLAZING SADDLES

1

THE 1970S: ANYTHING GOES

On June 12, 1972, a little film called *Deep Throat* premiered at the World Theater in New York City. The movie quickly went on to make a record (for the time) $3 million in its first six weeks of release, leading it to be referred to as "The *Ben-Hur* of porn flicks," and it became a sensation that helped to launch a middle-class, all-American interest in porn movies that came to be called "porno chic."

For the first time ever, Americans went to mainstream theaters in droves to see hard-core films that featured explicit sex; this was no longer just the "raincoat crowd," but rather young couples, older folks, and pretty much anyone who could get into the theater to see X-rated films. This trend did not arise out of a vacuum; it had been gestating for a while.

American and international films had been doing a slow striptease ever since the postwar era, but in the United States in particular, since 1952 when the U.S. Supreme Court declared film to be protected speech under the First Amendment in a case that had to do with the screening in New York State of the Italian film *The Miracle*, a short directed by Roberto Rossellini. The film, which was one half of an anthology movie called *L'Amore*, had been controversial in its depiction of a peasant girl who slept with a man she took to be Saint Joseph and ended up bearing his child. The National Legion of Decency and various Catholic organizations declared it to be blasphemy, but the court recognized the artistry of the film (which had been previously released in Italy, one of the most Catholic countries in the world, without incident) and declared it—and, by extension, films in general—to be artistic expression that was protected by the First Amendment. This opened the floodgates for foreign films containing subject matter that had long been banned under the U.S. Production Code to be released in America en masse.

The postwar years in America saw a gradual liberalization of culture in general, which ultimately led to the abandonment of the production code in 1968. The code was replaced with a rating system that consisted of four types of cinema: G, for general audiences; M (later PG) for more mature viewers; R (restricted to those over sixteen unless accompanied by an adult); and X, for those over sixteen only. Now, formerly taboo subjects such as prostitution, homosexuality, abortion, and other adult topics could be fully explored on-screen, with full-frontal nude scenes and the utterance of four-letter words as well.

The other arts were also becoming "liberated," with Broadway shows such as *Hair* and off-Broadway revues such as *Oh! Calcutta!* featuring nudity and strong language galore. The 1960s, after all, had been a time of revolution and challenges to societal norms, with Americans protesting the Vietnam War, women protesting for their own civil rights, and African Americans working hard to achieve theirs. The arts reflected these mercurial social changes as barriers were being broken down in every area of culture, not just in the United States but all over the free world.

Although television was still considered to be a family medium—at least in the United States—and therefore nudity and strong language were still forbidden, TV stretched the boundaries and pushed the envelope as much as possible. *Rowan and Martin's Laugh-In*, a wild sketch comedy series that started its run in 1968 and was hosted by comedians Dan Rowan and Dick Martin, became a cultural phenomenon for its poking fun at politics, its slightly off-color (and off-kilter) humor, and its ensemble cast of future stars, including Goldie Hawn, Lily Tomlin, and Richard Dawson.

All in the Family, an American sitcom debuting in 1971, was another breakthrough in its depiction of the life of a so-called lovable bigot named Archie Bunker, played to the hilt by Carroll O'Connor. Based on the British series *'Til Death Do Us Part*, the American version featured episodes centered around racism, infidelity, rape, homosexuality, and many other topics that were being explored on U.S. television for the first time.

American audiences were also amused by another first on *All in the Family:* the sound of a flushing toilet could be heard in the background in one scene of the first episode. This "rudeness" was accepted by sitcom audiences for the first time as a part of daily life that simply added to the realism of the televised life at the Bunkers' house. And it was a foreshadowing of "rudeness" to come in both comedies and dramas on television and in movie theaters.

It was in this cultural stew of the early seventies that comic, writer, and more recently, film director Mel Brooks decided to make his wildest film yet. Brooks, born on a tenement kitchen table as Melvin James Kaminsky in Brooklyn on June 28, 1926, came from a family of Jews from Kyiv, in what is now Ukraine. He had three older brothers: Lenny,

Bernie, and Irving. His father, Max, passed away of tuberculosis at the age of thirty-four. Brooks was only two years old at the time. Brooks said in later years that he felt that his father's early death was responsible for what he called his "anger and hostility" on which he based much of his comedy.

Brooks was a rather small child who had a tendency to be somewhat sickly, and he was bullied by other boys because of his size. Growing up in a tenement in the Brooklyn neighborhood of Williamsburg, Brooks had something of an epiphany when his uncle Joe took him to see the Broadway musical *Anything Goes*, starring Ethel Merman, at the Alvin Theater on West 52nd Street. Upon seeing the show, he informed his uncle that he wasn't going to work in the garment district like everyone else; he was going into show business.

Sure enough, when he was only fourteen, he got a job as a poolside entertainer in the summer resort area known as the Borscht Belt, located in the Catskill Mountains of upstate New York. At the hotel where he was performing, entertaining the guests around the pool by jumping into it with his clothes on and other wild physical comedy, he met an eighteen-year-old named Isaac "Sid" Caesar, who played in a dance band and performed comedy three times a week. They became fast friends. That same year, Brooks was also introduced to drummer and bandleader Buddy Rich, who taught him how to play the drums. Brooks started to earn money as a musician and, ultimately, got into performing stand-up comedy professionally when he was sixteen and had to step in at the last minute for an ailing emcee. It was around this time that Melvin James Kaminsky changed his professional name to Mel Brooks, taking his new surname from his mother's maiden name of Brookman.

After graduating high school in 1944, Brooks was drafted into the army and was sent to France and Belgium during World War II, ultimately participating in the Battle of the Bulge, the last major German offensive campaign on the Western Front during the war. After the war ended in Europe, Brooks joined the Special Services as a comic, where he toured army bases and was eventually put in charge of entertainment at Wiesbaden. In 1946, having attained the rank of corporal, Brooks was honorably discharged from the army.

Back home, Brooks's mother had gotten him a job at the Brooklyn Navy Yard, but the budding comic wanted no part of that. Instead, he headed back to the Catskills, where he worked as a stand-up comic, and began doing summer stock and radio work as well. When he was twenty-four, his old pal Sid Caesar offered him money to write gags for him, and Brooks became a full-time comedy writer.

He broke into the new medium of television—"the wave of the future"—with the help of Caesar, who hired him to write jokes for the DuMont/NBC series *The Admiral Broadway Revue* in 1949. Brooks received the princely salary of $50 a week—off the books. In 1950, Caesar created *Your Show of Shows*, a live ninety-minute variety show with an accent on comedy, for which he hired Brooks as one of the writers. The other writers included such future comedy greats as Carl Reiner, Neil Simon, and Mel Tolkin.

Sid Caesar's variety series *Your Show of Shows* ran from 1950 through 1954. His fellow writers on that series were Woody Allen, Neil Simon, Larry Gelbart, and Carl Reiner. *Your Show of Shows* was a huge success, only ending when costar Imogene Coca left the series to host her own series, *The Imogene Coca Show*, which ended up running for only one year.

Meanwhile, Caesar countered with *Caesar's Hour*, retaining most of his *Your Show of Shows* writers, including Brooks. *Caesar's Hour* ran from 1954 to 1957, and during the run, Brooks and Carl Reiner became close friends and worked out a few comic gags of their own. With Reiner, Brooks played the comic character "The 2,000 Year Old Man," in which Reiner interviewed Brooks's character for a series of comedy routines that were released on record and performed frequently on television. By the late 1950s, the frequently satirical act gained many admirers in New York City, including critic Kenneth Tynan, who called Brooks "the most original comic improvisor I had ever seen."

Brooks turned his talents to Broadway in the early 1960s when he wrote the music and lyrics to the show *All-American*, which debuted in 1962. Starring Ray Bolger, it ran for eighty performances and was nominated for two Tony Awards. In 1963, Brooks conceived an animated short comedy film called *The Critic*, a satire of so-called art films. Directed by Ernest Pintoff, it won the Academy Award for Best Animated Short Film.

At this point, Brooks went from strength to strength, combining talents with comedy writer Buck Henry to create *Get Smart*, a TV series about a bumbling spy, as a parodic answer to the spy craze that had currently taken over the pop culture landscape, a result of the huge success of the James Bond series that had begun with *Dr. No* (1962) and hit its peak with *Goldfinger* (1964). The Bond movies had made a star out of Sean Connery, and *Get Smart* did the same thing for former stand-up comic Don Adams. Beginning in 1965, *Get Smart* was a huge success on NBC and its zany, anarchic humor was tremendously influential, setting the stage for such wild series as *Rowan and Martin's Laugh-In*, which began three years later. *Get Smart* ran for five years and won seven Emmy Awards.

This all led to Brooks becoming a film director in 1967 with *The Producers*, a brazen satire of Broadway musicals that included the hilarious but controversial song, "Springtime for Hitler." The genesis for the film went all the way back to *All-American*, when a reporter asked Brooks what he was going to do next and he quipped, "Springtime for Hitler," the title of which may have been a spoof on *Springtime for Henry*, a comedy play that had scored an eight-month run on Broadway in the early 1930s. For several years, Brooks had considered a rather bold idea of writing a musical comedy that had something to do with Adolf Hitler. Eventually he found two brave producers, Joseph E. Levine and Sidney Glazier, and he ended up directing what came to be known as *The Producers*. Starring Zero Mostel and Gene Wilder, the film became an underground hit and won Best Original Screenplay for Brooks at the 41st annual Academy Awards.

Brooks's next feature film, *The Twelve Chairs* (1970), didn't fare so well. Loosely based on a Russian novel, the movie starred Ron Moody, Frank Langella, and Dom DeLuise and was filmed in Yugoslavia on a budget of $1.5 million. The comic story concerned three men in search of a set of twelve chairs that contained a fortune in diamonds. Despite the excellent cast, the film didn't do well with either the critics or the public and, for a short time, Brooks felt that his newly launched career as a film director was already over.

Several things conspired to make his next film a big hit, however. In 1972, Brooks met agent David Begelman, who helped to set up a deal with him at Warner Brothers in which he would be hired as a "script doctor" for an unproduced comedy-western called *Tex X*. Brooks was ultimately hired as director for the project, which would become one of the most successful comedy movies of all time.

The screenplay for *Tex X*, written by Andrew Bergman, was a parody of the western genre; the title was a reference to 1960s black Muslim leader Malcolm X, as it concerned a black sheriff in the Old West. Begelman told Brooks that it was perfect for him, and Brooks got together with Bergman, lawyer Norman Steinberg, dentist Alan Uger—and one other writer, comic Richard Pryor—to create what would eventually become *Blazing Saddles*, which not only spoofed westerns but, to a certain extent, made fun of so-called blaxploitation films.

The trend in the early seventies toward movies and television shows to explore previously untouched topics had led to a spate of films referred to as "blaxploitation." An ethnic subgenre of the action/exploitation film, blaxploitation coincided with the surge of social and political interest in race relations in the sixties and seventies, and the films were aimed at urban African American audiences, although the trend eventually expanded across racial and ethnic boundaries. Such films as *Cotton Comes to Harlem* (1970), *Shaft* (1971), and *Blacula* (1972) were essentially African American versions of tried-and-true Hollywood genres such as the detective film and the horror movie, but set in updated urban environments and featuring soul and funk music on the soundtrack.

Elements of blaxploitation eventually spilled over into other genres: the first James Bond movie to star Roger Moore, *Live and Let Die* (1973), was partially set in the Harlem underworld as well as in the voodoo cults of the West Indies. The martial arts movie *Enter the Dragon* paired Bruce Lee with black actor Jim Kelly in that same year.

This was not a time of what we would now called political correctness. Some blaxploitation films had titles that couldn't even be hinted at today. Movies such as *The Legend of N----r Charley* (1972) and *Boss N----r* (1975) pushed the envelope of what was acceptable even at that time. Can you imagine a theater marquee with the N-word emblazoned across it in the twenty-first century? Interestingly enough, both of those films were blaxploitation versions of that most classic of Hollywood genres, the western.

Tex X was also a western, albeit a comic one with a difference. As Brooks wrote in his autobiography *All About Me: My Remarkable Life in Show Business*, "The script was, in fact, crazy! The dialogue was 1974, and the setting was 1874. . . . Since this story was about a Black sheriff in a white western town, I knew I needed Richard Pryor to be one of the writers. He was a friend and a brilliant comedian who hadn't really broken out yet."

Brooks and his compatriots were about to create one of the most laugh-out-loud, outrageous, and politically incorrect comedies ever made.

2

"PLEASE DO NOT WRITE A POLITE SCRIPT"

Born to a Jewish family in Queens, New York in 1945, Andrew Bergman graduated from Binghamton University when he was twenty and attained his PhD in American history from the University of Wisconsin–Madison in 1970. The following year, Bergman published his first book, *We're in the Money: Depression America and Its Films* at NYU Press. The book took a detailed look at American films of the 1930s and of how they helped to keep alive the truths—and myths—of American society through one of its darkest periods in history. Bergman's writing style—which one critic noted "makes history fun"—ensured that the book was well received, and the author returned with another book about classic American movies, *James Cagney: The Pictorial Treasury of Film Stars*, published by Galahad Press early in 1974.

In between the writing of those books, however, Bergman broke into the film business by writing an original script called *Tex X*. Originally a novella about a black sheriff in the Old West, he sold the idea to Warner Brothers, and the studio asked him to turn it into a screenplay. The rest may be history, but it's a long and convoluted one.

That history shifted into high gear when Brooks got involved. It all came about as a result of Brooks meeting with David Begelman, a successful talent agent who had just joined forces with Freddie Fields—another successful talent agent—to form Creative Management Associates (CMA), which represented Brooks. As Brooks wrote in his autobiography, at this time in his career he had two Oscars and plenty of critical acclaim, but he had only earned $50,000 apiece for *The Producers* and *The Twelve Chairs*, and he was wondering if he'd be able to make a living making films.

Begelman was a fan of Brooks's work and one day in 1973, he happened to bump into him on 57th Street in New York. Begelman asked Brooks to join him for lunch. It turned out to be a fateful meeting. As Brooks wrote in his memoirs, "I knew he would take me to a good place for lunch because he dressed well, drove a Rolls Royce, and generally lived in style."

Begelman took Brooks to the dining room of the Sherry-Netherlands Hotel and, over lunch, pointed out to Brooks that he had just placed a call to him that hadn't been returned. Brooks said he would probably receive the call when he got home and asked Begelman what it was about. Begelman said, "It's about a rough draft of a movie that I just read. It's a movie you were born to make." The agent went on to tell him that the script was zany, "all over the place," and that there was some wonderful stuff in it.

Brooks pointed out that he always wrote and directed his own work and that he wasn't really for hire. Begelman was insistent, however; he went on to say that this project could be very commercial, and that he could probably get Brooks $100,000 to rewrite and direct it. As Brooks was not at the top of his game financially at that time, he told Begelman he might rethink things; he might be for hire after all!

Begelman took Brooks back to his office at CMA and handed him the rough draft of the *Tex X* screenplay. He asked him to take it to the next office to read it, come back and they would discuss it. As it turned out, Brooks was enchanted by the script. As he put it, "The dialogue was 1974, and the setting was 1874. It was right up my alley. I knew it was the beginning of something that could be very, very good."

Brooks told Begelman that he wanted to rework the script with a group of comedy writers, because that was the way he was used to working on the Sid Caesar shows. Begelman agreed and hired him to write and direct *Tex X* on the spot. Brooks wanted to retain Bergman, as he didn't want to drop the writer who came up with the idea, feeling that he could continue to be very important to the screenplay.

After hiring Bergman for the rewrite, Brooks went directly to his friend Richard Pryor. He felt that Pryor was not only the best stand-up comic who ever lived, but that he was the perfect writer for this movie because "his comedy came from the humanity that he had experienced."

In the early seventies, Pryor was just about to break through to mainstream audiences. Born in Peoria, Illinois in 1970, Pryor had grown up in a brothel run by his grandmother, where his alcoholic mother worked as a prostitute. His father was a former boxer, hustler, and pimp. Pryor's mother had abandoned him when he was ten years old, leaving him to be raised by his violent, abusive grandmother. He was one of four children raised in the brothel, and he was sexually abused when he was seven years old.

The unusual circumstances of Pryor's upbringing—which included frequent beatings by his grandmother—caused him to act out in school, and he was expelled at age fourteen. Pryor joined the army in 1958, where he served until 1960. Stationed in West Germany, he continued his tendency toward volatility, and was briefly jailed there for an incident in which he and several other black soldiers beat and stabbed—although not fatally—a white soldier for laughing at the racially charged scenes in the film *Imitation of Life*, in which director Douglas Sirk examined the issues of class, race, and gender.

In 1963, determined to make a name for himself that wouldn't be published only in the police blotter, Pryor moved to New York City and began performing in clubs alongside such performers as Nina Simone, Woody Allen, and Bob Dylan. Inspired by the success of rising African American comic Bill Cosby, Pryor began his career in comedy as a mainstream act, eschewing any real controversy at first. He appeared on such middle-brow, all-American television shows as *The Ed Sullivan Show*, *The Tonight Show*, and *The Merv Griffin Show*, leading to a successful stint in Las Vegas. His wordplay and hilarious stories led to a steady if unspectacular early career in which he even did some acting on TV series such as *The Wild Wild West*.

In 1967, eager to spice up his act, he sensed the zeitgeist of the times and started adding profanity to his wordplay, often using the verboten N-word in reference to himself. Two years later, he moved to Berkeley, California, where he became immersed in the counterculture, explored his bisexuality (he once allegedly had an affair with Marlon Brando, among others), and started writing for television series such as *Sanford and Son* and a special starring Lily Tomlin for which he shared an Emmy Award. He also expanded his acting résumé in such films as *Lady Sings the Blues* (1972) and *The Mack* (1973).

He already had two comedy albums to his credit at the independent label Laff Records when he released his breakthrough album *That N----r's Crazy* in 1974. It was a commercial and critical hit, winning the Grammy Award for Best Comedy Album in 1975. When Brooks contacted him to work on *Tex X*, Pryor was on the cusp of stardom. He was also, unfortunately, prey to a pretty expensive cocaine habit, among other forms of substance abuse.

Brooks noted years later that, during the writing process for *Tex X*, all the writers would meet for breakfast every morning, scarfing down bagels and lox. They would wash down breakfast with heavy doses of coffee, but Pryor would dose his with something extra: Remy Martin, a very good French brandy. Whether that sort of indulgence either helped or hurt Pryor's contributions remains an open question that will probably never be answered.

Brooks hired two more writers for the film: one was an attorney named Norman Steinberg, who was an aspiring writer. He had a friend, a dentist named Alan Uger, who was his writing partner. As Brooks admitted in his memoirs, "I just loved the idea of having a comedy writing team that included a lawyer and a dentist. They were just so wrong, they were absolutely right!"

Brooks hadn't worked with a writing team since *Your Show of Shows* with Sid Caesar. To spur on his writers, and to give them an idea of what he wanted from them, Brooks posted a large sign outside the writer's room which read "Please do not write a polite script." On the inside wall, he posted—in large print—FIRST WE LAUGH.

Years later Brooks described the writing as, shall we say, chaotic: "*Blazing Saddles* was more or less written in the middle of a drunken fistfight. There were five of us, all yelling loudly for our ideas to be put into the movie. Not only was I the loudest, but luckily, I also had the right as director to decide what was in or out."

In 2016, Andrew Bergman told Brock Swanson of *Creative Screenwriting Magazine*, "In the beginning, we had five people. One guy left in a couple of weeks. Then it was basically me, Mel, Richie Pryor, and Norman Steinberg. Richie left after the first draft and then Norman, Mel and I wrote the next three or four drafts. It was a riot. It was a rioter's room!"

Brooks said that, while working on the script, there was no subject that he felt was "untouchable." If he or the other writers thought of something, no matter how crazy, or "socially unacceptable," they'd throw it into the mix, because if it came into their minds, it was worth talking about. According to Brooks, "The tone I set for the writing team was the freedom that comes from having nothing to lose. . . . We had absolutely no restrictions on any and all subjects."

To further illustrate what it's like to collaborate with Mel Brooks, Steve Haberman, co-screenwriter of *Life Stinks* (1991) and *Dracula: Dead and Loving It* (1995) was interviewed for this book. Haberman, who has a doctorate in film, has known Brooks for a long time. He told me that he went to the University of Southern California for his cinematic degree and that he had impressed his professors with a short film he made called *Blind Curves*.

> I was fortunate enough to have this professor, Dr. Black, a writing teacher who made an impression on me. He had taught Robert Zemeckis and John Milius and George Lucas and so many others. He liked my work and got me an agent at William Morris when I was still at USC. So I was actually

getting screenplays optioned when I was still a student at USC, an undergraduate.

I made this movie *Blind Curves* outside of USC, and I put it in a film festival and I won. Somebody saw it, a guy named Don Behrns, who I think was a production manager on John Carpenter's *Halloween*. Anyway, at that time, he was working for New World after Roger Corman left. They were making all these B-movies for drive-ins, which were big in those days. They saw *Blind Curves* and they liked it, and they had this breakdancing musical called *Body Rock* and this very nice guy named Marcello Epstein was supposed to direct it. I think he wrote the script too. Anyway, he had done music videos and but he'd never done a feature, so they hired me to be a visual consultant, or pictorial consultant, however you want to say it. So my job was to read the script, go on location scouts with him, and break the script down into shots with him and storyboard it. So I did that and he let me on the set every day, and one day we were doing a big dance number and it was, like, guys in skeleton costumes and fog in a studio in Santa Monica. He didn't really have time to finish it. And the DP [director of photography], this guy named Robby Muller—I don't know how they got him, but he was Wim Wenders' great DP—said, "I don't think we can cover this," and we had to go to LAX [Los Angeles Airport] in the afternoon and catch a plane to go to New York to film the exteriors. The movie was supposed to take place in New York, right?

So I said, "I've got an idea. Let's put the camera on a crane and we'll do the rehearsal"—because I had worked with the choreographer to storyboard the dance routine—"we'll run through the dance, and I will block where the crane is going to stop. And everywhere the crane stops, we'll do cross angles that we can cut to, because we probably won't be able to get the whole thing in one crane shot. So let's do that, let's put it on the crane, see how far we get moving with the dancers and we'll get the star, Lorenzo Lamas. . . . "

So we did that, we put the camera on the crane, we did the whole thing, and we got it. And we had time to go back and mark it on the stage and do cross angles, and we'd cut the best parts of the moving crane shots together. We got it in time to uncork champagne before everybody had to get on the bus and go to LAX to fly to New York. The very next day, we were going to start shooting location stuff.

The day that I did that, it just so happened that Chuck Russell, who was the executive producer—who went on to direct *Mask* and *A Nightmare on Elm Street 3*—was there and saw me do this. Also, the head of New World was there, so they all saw me do this, right? And ever after, when they had a director they didn't feel comfortable with, someone who came from commercials or sitcoms or something besides features, they would hire me to be the visual consultant—basically a job I made up.

I ended up working on B-movies like *Once Bitten* and *Return to Horror High*. So one day I got a call from my agent to work on a film called *Transylvania 6-5000*. The director is a guy named Rudy De Luca; he's a writer for Mel Brooks, and I'd get to go to Yugoslavia for this movie with this great cast including Jeff Goldblum and Ed Begley and Geena Davis and Carol Kane. A big cast. The day I was there, he was auditioning Michael Richards, who later played Kramer on *Seinfeld*. So Rudy hires me as a consultant and we go to Yugoslavia and we make this movie in a real castle in a town outside the village of Zagreb, which has cobblestone streets and gothic architecture; it's perfect.

So we make this movie, and Rudy has no business directing a movie; he couldn't direct anyone to the bathroom. So we come back to the States and the movie comes out and it's a hit. I think the budget was like $3 million and it makes more than $9 million. Rudy's writing partner was Barry Levinson. They'd been writing together for three years and had won two Emmys for *The Carol Burnett Show*. They had co-written *Silent Movie* and *High Anxiety*. Barry had gone off to direct *Diner*, which wasn't a hit, but it was a critical hit. I think he was directing *The Natural* at the time, with Robert Redford. So Rudy said to me when we came back to the States, "Do you want to be my writing partner?" I said sure. I'm a kid, and this guy had Emmys and had worked with Mel Brooks. So Rudy and I got together and worked on a bunch of stuff, and one day, we're at Rudy's house and the phone rings; it's Mel Brooks. He had just done *Spaceballs*, and he asked Rudy, "Do you have anything?" And Rudy said no. And Mel said, "Well, I don't have anything either." And I said, "I have something!"

And so, I go into Mel's office at 20th Century Fox, a big office on the corner, Dick Powell's old office on the second floor. And I pitch him this movie. And Mel likes it; right away, he likes it. He slaps the table and says, "We'll make it!" And so we make *Life Stinks*. And Mel is very happy with *Life Stinks*, even though it didn't do very well, because he's got a great part in it and it's really the only movie he's made since *The Twelve Chairs* that's not a parody. It was actually a movie that he cared about.

I figured out that Mel was an *auteur*. This was news to Mel. But he made movies about people with wild schemes, usually a pair of men. Not that he's gay; he's not. But it's usually two guys who have no business being together and they team up to do something crazy, and they pull it off. And so I thought it would be interesting if a rich guy and a homeless guy did something together. And I thought about it, and I showed Mel movies like *Sullivan's Travels* and Chaplin movies and stuff like that, and we talked about it being a rich man and a homeless woman. And so we worked on it and it became *Life Stinks*.

With De Luca assisting Brooks and Haberman on the screenplay, *Life Stinks* costarred Lesley Ann Warren as Molly, the homeless woman who ends up teaching Brooks's character—an empathy-free CEO of a large corporation—about what's really important in life. A more down-to-earth and poignant movie than most of Brooks's films up to that time, *Life Stinks* was neither a critical nor a box-office success, but Haberman and Brooks hit it off as a writing team.

"Mel has his writers around every second," Haberman explained,

from pre-production through production through post-production . . . and when the movie was all done, he said to me, "You know a lot about movies. I'm not just Mel Brooks; I'm a very classy guy who produced *The Elephant Man* and *The Fly*, *84 Charing Cross Road* and a lot of classy movies, and I think you should make a movie for Brooksfilms." So I wrote this science-fiction/horror movie called *Not Human*, and Mel bought it, God bless him. And he started to set it up and we worked on it for a long time, doing storyboards and set design; it had a monster, all this stuff. And one day he called me up and said, "We're going to make *Not Human* but it's now being called *Species* and you're not involved." So that sort of crushed that dream.

But while I was working on *Not Human*, Rudy and I also came up with a script called *Dracula: Dead and Liking It*. And we decided to let Mel read it, so we brought it in on one of our meetings on *Not Human* and he puts it on his desk. So I'm coming in once a week for *Not Human*, and I notice that the script is in the same place on Mel's desk as when I gave it to him. So I said, "Mel, you gotta read this!" And he said, "Yeah, I'll read it."

So one night at 9:30, the phone rings . . . and I pick it up and it's Mel. He said, "I read *Dracula*. We're gonna make it! I'm playing Van Helsing! Lunch tomorrow!" Click. So that was the beginning of that adventure.

So we made *Dracula*, which was finally called *Dracula: Dead and Loving It*. And when that was done, he asked me to write something cheaper than *Not Human*, so I wrote a little horror movie called *Pizza Man* and he bought that too. And that never got made either. And in the meantime, I got a PhD in film and I've done a bunch of audio commentaries and have written three books.

Haberman pointed out that he loves *both* versions of *The Producers*, as well as *The Twelve Chairs*, *Blazing Saddles*, *Young Frankenstein*, and all the others. He said that when collaborating with Brooks,

> We're all in the same room. If you sell him stories or screenplays . . . if film is an art, then I think it has to have an artist. Many films are works of studio collaboration—*Gone with the Wind*, *Casablanca*, stuff like that—but for me, the great films are the works of one really strong visionary. And Mel is like that. Even though I've written many scripts with Mel Brooks—even ones that got made that you didn't know I was involved with, as well as ones that didn't get made—he insists on things if he's the director and the producer and the star. You can change his mind and you can lobby for things, but in the end, you have to give it to Mel because it's a Mel Brooks movie. The movie is getting made because Mel Brooks wants to make it.
>
> So, even though we worked together on what became known as *Dracula: Dead and Loving It*, when I said I didn't want certain elements—I wanted the comedy to come from the characters and the subject matter—that wasn't saying that I didn't want it to be a Mel Brooks movie. I still wanted it to be his vision, because he's more than just some of his stylistic tics; he's very profound and very warm. Much warmer than me. He has a very warm vision of people. He's like Fellini in a way; he's

very critical, he's very satirical, but he's also like a big bear hug. He likes people. The big difference between Mel and me is that he likes people and I don't. You can see that in his comedy.

Haberman noted that Brooks has that kind of warm approach to comedy in common with Sid Caesar:

I actually worked with Sid Caesar, believe it or not. So I know firsthand what Sid was like. Sid was going to do a show for CBS called *The Sid Caesar Show*. He hired Rudy and me as his head writers. I worked with Sid; the three of us worked together on these scripts. So I know what Mel went through, and I know how Mel became Mel.

Sid is not a warm guy in person. But his comedy is also very humanistic. It's very much based on observations of the human comedy."

I asked Haberman if Brooks was a tough taskmaster, and his response was this:

I would say he's not a taskmaster. He doesn't crack the whip, but he's very firm about what he wants and what he doesn't want. If he likes a joke, it's in. When you work with Sid and you come up with something that makes him laugh, he goes into character right there, and you get a little Sid Caesar performance right there in the room, and it's brilliant. He was the greatest sketch comic who ever lived. And Mel sometimes does that, but sometimes he just laughs along with you. We laugh, and then he'll add another joke or sometimes try the opposite of your joke, and you go back and forth and you eventually land on what's going to be in the movie.

Sometimes you wish that, for God's sake, he'd let you put one of your jokes in the movie, but he just firmly doesn't want to do it; and not just jokes in the movie, but story points and casting and everything else, because, remember, he has us there with him all the time, he discusses everything with us. We go on auditions with him and everything.

Haberman's belief in the *auteur* theory means that, when working with Brooks, he has to check his own ego at the door: "I think when we work together, that I'm only a part of Mel's vision. I wouldn't have made a movie like *Life Stinks* . . . but Mel did. Even though I came up with the story, in my opinion, it was just a clever story idea. But he brought the warmth to it, and he brought the love for the people to it. We both came up with the comedy, but his comedy was very embracing."

But back to *Blazing Saddles*: To a certain extent, the film's plot echoed that of *The Producers* in that it concerned a money-making scheme, as well as two male partners who, as Haberman noted, were polar opposites. In the Old West, circa 1874, a corrupt politician named Hedley Lamarr comes up with a plan to ruin the town of Rock Ridge so they can get the land cheaply to profit off the incoming transcontinental railroad. Part of the grift involves appointing a black sheriff, under the assumption that the townspeople will pack up and get out of town when they see him. It doesn't work out that way, however, and the new sheriff, "Black Bart," who teams up with a washed-up gunslinger, ends up becoming very popular with Rock Ridge's citizens and

Lamarr's nemesis, turning the tables on Lamarr and saving the town from disaster.

As Brooks put it, it was a pretty basic western plot (except for the racial elements), but the decision was to "stand it on its ear," throwing in off-the-wall comedy routines. As he insisted, nothing was off-limits, no matter how crazy; at one point, there are even references to Bugs Bunny (as Warner Brothers owned the character, that was fine with them) and to another Warners property, *The Treasure of the Sierra Madre* (1948).

Brooks's *auteur* theory of comedy, however, went beyond mere zaniness. He felt that you had to have an "engine" driving the wacky bits, a more serious and down-to-earth backstory. In the case of *Tex X*, that backstory had to do with racism. As Brooks opined, "Racial prejudice is the engine that really drives the film and helps to make it work."

Six months after their first writing session, the screenwriters had forged a rough draft, the title of which was changed from *Tex X* to avoid having it confused with an X-rated movie. It was now called *Black Bart*, a title that Brooks still wasn't entirely happy with. He felt that it wasn't crazy enough and failed to inform audiences what the film was really about.

After toying with such generic titles as *Purple Sage*, Brooks claimed that he came up with the final moniker for the movie while he was taking a shower. According to Brooks, "It hit me. *Blazing Saddles*. Two western clichés, 'blazing' and 'saddles.' No one had ever put them together and for good reason—they simply don't go together. However, they cry 'Crazy Western!' and that's what we were making. . . . The title tells you everything."

Brooks felt that his crazy western should please two distinct audiences: film buffs who got all the in-jokes and a more general audience that just came to laugh. Brooks tried not to weigh down any of his parodies with too many "arcane" references. As he put it, the only requirement for any Mel Brooks comedy is that you come to laugh.

With the rough draft completed, Brooks and the remaining two other writers—Bergman and Steinberg—set off for Hollywood to continue to polish the screenplay. The gestation of *Blazing Saddles* was taking some time, but it would prove to be worth the wait.

3

THE PROBLEMS WITH PRYOR
... AND CASTING

According to Brooks, when casting began, "it was daunting." Their first obstacle was in casting the lead role of the black sheriff. Naturally enough, Brooks and his compatriots wanted Richard Pryor to play the part. Warner Bros., however, balked at the idea. According to Brooks, the studio heads "were afraid of his erratic behavior," but there was more to it than that. They were all too aware of his checkered past, and they claimed that his record of drug arrests made him uninsurable. No matter how much Brooks begged, Warner Bros. stood their ground and gave him a firm "no," refusing to finance the picture if Pryor was the star.

Although he was disappointed—but perhaps not surprised—Pryor stayed on as screenwriter, happy to take the credit for some of *Blazing Saddles*' bawdiest moments. Would *Blazing Saddles* have been even funnier if Pryor had played the lead? We'll never know.

And so Brooks was back to square one. Who would play Sheriff Bart? Brooks looked around until he found someone "who was made for the part and born to play it." That someone was Broadway actor Cleavon Little, who had won a Tony Award and a Drama Desk Award for starring in *Purlie*, a musical written by Ossie Davis, Philip Rose, Peter Udell, and Gary Geld.

Cleavon Jake Little was born in Chickasha, Oklahoma, in 1939. He was the brother of DeEtta Little West, a singer who is now best known for her performance with Nelson Pigford on the vocals for Bill Conti's "Gonna Fly Now" from the movie *Rocky* (1976). Raised in San Diego, California, Little graduated from Kearny High School in 1957. He later attended San Diego State College, where he graduated with a degree in speech therapy.

Little decided early on that he wanted to be an actor. His first stage appearance was in *A Raisin in the Sun* in 1962 at San Diego's Old Globe Theatre. He won a scholarship from the American Broadcasting Company (ABC) to attend the American Academy of Dramatic Arts in Manhattan, where he was named best actor in the class of 1967. Little made his professional acting debut in February of that year as the Muslim Witch in *Macbird*, a satire written by Barbara Garson that was a mash-up of events from the John F. Kennedy assassination with Shakespeare's *Macbeth*. It was performed off-Broadway at the Village Gate, a nightclub in Greenwich Village. In October 1967, Little appeared as Foxtrot in Bruce Jay Friedman's play *Scuba Duba*.

Little spent much of 1967 performing at the New York Shakespeare Festival, where he played *Hamlet*. He made his first film appearance the following year in George Seaton's *What's So Bad about Feeling Good?* in which he essayed a small, uncredited role. Several tiny roles ensued in such films as *John and Mary* (1969) and *Cotton Comes to Harlem* (1970). He also appeared on TV in two episodes of the ABC series *Felony Squad*.

Little's Broadway debut was in 1969, as Lee Haines in the musical *Jimmy Shine*, written by John Sebastian and Murray Schisgal. The title role was played by none other than Dustin Hoffman. In 1970, after his flirtation with movies and television, he returned to Broadway to play the title role in *Purlie*.

The following year, Little appeared in *The David Frost Revue*, a satirical series featuring an ensemble cast that included Dom DeLuise, Marcia Rodd, and Jack Gilford. Also in 1971, Little was cast as the blind radio announcer Super Soul in Richard C. Sarafian's *Vanishing Point*, costarring Barry Newman and Dean Jagger. During that very busy year, he also appeared as a preacher in the pilot film for *The Waltons*, which was titled *The Homecoming: A Christmas Story* on CBS-TV. He also played a burglar in a 1971 episode of *All in the Family*.

Little's highest-profile part in those days was as the star of an ABC sitcom called *Temperatures Rising*, which also featured James Whitmore and Joan Van Ark, from 1972 to 1974. The series aired in three different formats with various casts during its relatively short run, with Little as the only continuing character throughout all the format changes.

With appearances in such television series as *The Six Million Dollar Man*, Little found himself going from strength to strength and he caught the attention of Brooks, who asked him to come in and read for the part of Sheriff Bart. After Little read one page of dialogue, Brooks grabbed him, threw his arms around him and told him, "Cleavon, if you don't ask for too much money, you've got the part."

Even Pryor, still nursing his wounds from being turned down by the studio, agreed that Little was perfect for the role. When Brooks asked Pryor his thoughts on Little taking over the role, Pryor told him, "I could be Cuban, but there's no mistaking Cleavon; he'd scare the shit out of those rednecks!"

Now that Black Bart was agreed upon, the rest of the casting needed to be completed. Brooks felt that there was only one actress who could play Lili Von Shtüpp, a character based on "Frenchy," the saloon singer played by Marlene Dietrich in the classic western *Destry Rides Again* (1939). That actress was Madeline Kahn, whom Brooks had seen in her Broadway debut, *Leonard Sillman's New Faces of 1968*; he had followed her career ever since. Kahn was a versatile actress, comedian, and singer who had been born in Boston in 1942 and had earned a drama scholarship to Hofstra University on Long Island. As was the case with Cleavon Little, she graduated from college with a degree in speech therapy and she auditioned for professional stage roles shortly after graduation.

Kahn's film debut was in the short *De Duva (The Dove)* (1968), an Oscar-nominated parody of the films of director Ingmar Bergman. Her feature debut came about in the screwball Barbra Streisand comedy *What's Up, Doc?* (1972), in which she played Ryan O'Neal's fiancée, who was prone to fits of hysteria. Her film career really took off when she appeared in O'Neal's next movie, *Paper Moon* (1973), for which she received an Academy Award nomination for Best Supporting Actress.

Brooks had seen her in the latter two films and felt that she was an incredibly gifted actress in the areas of timing, voice, and attitude. As he wrote in his memoirs, "The camera was in love with her, and if she wanted to, she could have been a legitimate Metropolitan Opera singer. She had the pipes!"

Brooks told Kahn that she would be parodying Dietrich; there is a scene in *Destry Rides Again* in which Dietrich's character Frenchy straddles a chair while she sings "What the Boys in the Back Room Will Have," showing off her legs, which are clad in black stockings. When Kahn auditioned for the role, Brooks asked her to raise her skirt a bit so he could see her legs. According to Brooks, she said, "Oh, it's gonna be one of those auditions, eh?"

Brooks assured her that it was not, in fact, "one of those auditions," and that he just wanted to see if she could pull off the Dietrich parody. And so, according to Brooks, she pulled up a chair and showed him her Dietrich-like legs. He told her on the spot that she had the role.

Another all-important role was the villain of the piece, Hedley Lamarr. Brooks watched *The Carol Burnett Show* on TV for inspiration; it was there he found Harvey Korman, Burnett's costar and frequent foil on the beloved variety show. Born in Chicago in 1927, Korman was of Russian and Jewish descent who studied at the Goodman School of Drama at the Art Institute of Chicago. Some time later, he became a member of the Peninsula Players summer theater program during their 1950, 1957, and 1958 seasons. His first television role was a walk-on in a 1960 episode of *The Donna Reed Show*; and from there he went on to appear in episodes of such iconic sixties series as *Route 66*, *The Eleventh Hour*, and *Perry Mason*. From 1963 through 1967, he was a semi-regular on *The Danny Kaye Show*, and when that series ended, he segued into *The Carol Burnett Show*, for which he won four Emmy Awards and a Golden Globe. His first feature film role, oddly enough, came about in 1961 in a "nudie" exploitation film directed by schlockmeister Herschell Gordon Lewis (*Blood Feast*, 1963) called *Living Venus*. Korman played a fashion photographer in that epic, which was a thinly veiled biography of *Playboy* founder Hugh Hefner.

Although Korman's own series, *The Harvey Korman Show* (1977), only lasted five episodes, the actor found himself constantly in demand because of his reputation, what Brooks referred to as an "ever popular and talented laugh maker." When Brooks hired him for *Blazing Saddles*, he was in the middle of his hugely popular tenure on Burnett's series, which frequently paired him to hilarious effect with fellow *laughmeister* Tim Conway.

Brooks found Korman to be perfect for the role of the slick-talking conman Lamarr, in part because of what he referred to as his "classy Shakespearean tone," which added to his delivery as the character. *Blazing Saddles* turned out to be the first of many fruitful collaborations he would have with Korman.

The supporting roles were just as important to Brooks's vision. For "Lamarr's big dumb stupid foreman, Taggart," as he put it, he cast ubiquitous cowboy actor Slim Pickens. Born Louis Burton Lindley Jr. in 1919, Pickens—his stage name from the days when he was a rodeo performer—was, at one time, a member of the Future Farmers of America. He grew up on a dairy farm in California and, after serving a stint in the U.S. Army Air Force during World War II, he drifted into the acting business and made his film debut in the Errol Flynn western *Rocky Mountain* (1950). His distinctive features and country drawl made him a natural for oaters, and he appeared in dozens of them, where his rodeo background came in handy; he never needed a double for the horseback-riding scenes. His résumé of western movies was extensive, including such films as *One-Eyed Jacks* (1961), the 1966 remake of *Stagecoach*, and *The Cowboys* (1972). He was also featured in episodes of numerous western series on television, such as *Overland Trail* (1960), *The Outlaws* (1960–1962), and *Custer* (1967).

Pickens appeared in more than just westerns, however. In 1964, he played a particularly oily villain in an episode of *The Man From UNCLE*, and that same year featured him in what was perhaps his most famous role: Major T. J. "King" Kong in Stanley Kubrick's *Dr. Strangelove or: How I Learned to Stop Worrying and Love the Bomb*. The iconic scene in which he rides the bomb at the end of the film came about quite literally by accident when Peter Sellers—who was supposed to have played the role in addition to three other roles in the film—had to bow out of playing Kong after he sprained his ankle and was unable to work in the cramped cockpit set. Pickens was chosen for the role because of his accent and comic sensibilities, and he turned out to be perfect for the part of the B-52 pilot who was almost absurdly gung-ho. Pickens considered *Dr. Strangelove* to be a turning point in his career, and from then on he was much in demand for roles outside the western genre—particularly in comedy—including such classic TV series as *Mannix*, *The Mary Tyler Moore Show*, and *The Love Boat*.

For the character of Mongo—created by Pryor—"a big dumb brute" as Brooks described him, Brooks hired football player, professional wrestler, sportscaster, and sometime actor Alex Karras, who played with the Detroit Lions from 1958 to 1970. When the film version of George Plimpton's book *Paper Lion* was produced in 1968, Karras made his film debut portraying himself. His penchant for comedy led him to appear in an episode of *The Mary Tyler Moore Show*, a 1972 TV movie called *Hardcase*, and a 1973 TV movie called *The 500 Pound Jerk*. Brooks enjoyed Karras's sense of humor and hired him for the small but memorable role of Mongo, a slow-witted thug who was occasionally given to odd philosophical insights. According to Brooks, the role "fit Karras like a glove. (A big glove)."

One of the running gags in *Blazing Saddles* was that nearly everyone in the town of Rock Ridge had the surname Johnson. Olson Johnson (another in-joke: the character name was taken from the forties comedy team Olson and Johnson) was played by character actor David Huddleston, a frequent guest star on 1960s and 1970s television series such as *Adam-12*, *Then Came Bronson,* and *Bonanza*, and who was also in such western movies as *Rio Lobo* (1970) with John Wayne.

For the small but hilarious role of Reverend Johnson, Brooks cast Liam Dunn, who he had spotted in *What's Up, Doc?*, in which Kahn had also appeared. Brooks wanted to form a stock company of movie actors, and Dunn fit right in with his plans; the character actor had made a name for himself in various episodes of TV series such as *Room 222*, *Alias Smith and Jones*, and *Gunsmoke*. His comic timing was impeccable, and his role in *Blazing Saddles* would be the first of three times he would work with Brooks.

John Hillerman, best known as Jonathan Quayle Higgins III on *Magnum, P.I.* (1980–1988), in which he costarred with Tom Selleck, was cast as Howard Johnson. His role in that detective series made him seem like a fussy, pseudo-British character, but in fact Hillerman was born in Texas and served in the U.S. Air Force. His film debut came about in 1970 in *They Call Me Mister Tibbs!* in which he had an uncredited role as a reporter. Hillerman was yet another alumnus of *What's Up, Doc?* as well as *The Last Picture Show* (1971) and *Paper Moon.*

Familiar character actor George Furth portrayed Van Johnson; Furth was often cast as milquetoast-type characters in a wide variety of film and television roles, including *The Boston Strangler* (1968), *Butch Cassidy and the Sundance Kid* (1969), and *Myra Breckinridge* (1970). Furth was also a playwright, and he adapted his play *Twigs* as a 1975 television production starring Carol Burnett.

Jack Starrett was cast as Gabby Johnson, a parody of western movie sidekick George "Gabby" Hayes. Another Texan, Starrett was a veteran of then-popular "biker" films such as *The Born Losers*, *Hell's Angels on Wheels* (both 1967), and *Angels from Hell* (1968). He also directed two in the "cycle," so to speak: *Run, Angel, Run!* (1969) and *Nam's Angels* (1970). Later in his career, he helmed the well-regarded horror film *Race with the Devil* (1975), starring Peter Fonda and Warren Oates.

Character actress Carol Arthur was chosen to play outspoken schoolmarm Harriet Johnson. Arthur was the wife of Brooks's friend Dom DeLuise, who had previously starred in *The Twelve Chairs*. DeLuise also had a small role in *Blazing Saddles* as a character called "Buddy Bizarre."

Charles McGregor (Charlie) was an actor with, to say the least, a checkered past: he had served twenty-eight years in various prisons for two murders. Upon his release, he became an actor and counseled children on the pitfalls of crime, drugs, and incarceration. He was a supporting actor in a number of blaxploitation films, including *Super Fly*, *Across 110th Street* (both 1972), and *Hell Up in Harlem* (1974).

Pulchritude was provided by actress/model Robyn Hilton as Miss Stein, secretary to governor William J. Lepetomane (Brooks). That role was the voluptuous redhead's screen debut, and, while a small part, it was pretty hard to miss. She went on from there to appear, mostly as window dressing, in such sexploitation films as *The Single Girls*, *The Last Porno Flick* (both 1974), and *Video Vixens* (1975). Known mainly for her physical attributes, she was not afraid to show them in film, television, and magazines.

Towering six-feet, seven-inches tall, Don Megowan was cast in the small role of "Gum Chewer." In part because of his height, Megowan had played monsters in several fifties and sixties sci-fi and horror films, including *The Creature Walks among Us* (1956) and the Frankenstein monster in a failed TV pilot called *Tales of Frankenstein* (1958). He also had heroic roles in *The Werewolf* (1956) and *The Creation of the Human-oids* (1962). His western credits included *Davy Crockett, King of the Wild Frontier* (1955), *The Great Locomotive Chase* (1956), and episodes of TV series such as *Daniel Boone*.

Strangely enough—and in a typical Brooks touch—musician, band-leader, and composer Count Basie also shows up in *Blazing Saddles:* he and his orchestra make a cameo appearance in the desert playing "April in Paris" as Sheriff Bart rides toward Rock Ridge to assume his duties.

Other cameo roles included that of Robert Ridgely, doing a very good Boris Karloff impression as Boris the hangman, and an uncredited Ralph Manza as a man dressed as Hitler. Brooks wanted to ensure that every role, no matter how tiny, was memorably funny.

The toughest role to cast, though, was the other lead character, the Waco Kid, an alcoholic ex-gunslinger who ultimately finds redemption. In his autobiography, Brooks wrote that he wanted to cast either a well-known cowboy actor or a well-known alcoholic—or a combination of both. This led to more casting complications. His first choice would have been a very famous cowboy actor indeed, as we shall see in our next chapter.

4

WHO RIDES
A BLAZING SADDLE?

One fine day, Brooks was having lunch at the Warner Brothers studio commissary when he happened to look across the room to see none other than John Wayne sitting there. The iconic western star was on the Warners lot filming *The Train Robbers*, costarring Ann-Margret, Rod Taylor, Ben Johnson, and Ricardo Montalban, and was enjoying his own hearty lunch. Brooks suddenly had an epiphany and thought that it would be an inspiration—not to mention a stroke of luck—to cast Wayne as the Waco Kid. Ginning up his courage, Brooks got up and moseyed on over to Wayne's table, where he introduced himself. Wayne immediately recognized him. He laughed and informed Brooks that *The Producers* was one of his favorite comedies.

Wayne asked him, "So what are you making now?" Brooks explained the plot of *Blazing Saddles* in a nutshell and informed Wayne that the proposed movie broke all the rules of western movies, save one: the good guys triumphed in the end. Wayne liked the sound of that and asked Brooks to send the script to his office. He said he would read it that night and meet Brooks at the same table tomorrow at lunchtime.

Brooks was so ecstatic he could barely sleep that night. He couldn't get over his apparent stroke of good fortune. With Wayne parodying his own screen persona as the Waco Kid, *Blazing Saddles* would be virtually guaranteed of being a big hit.

Sadly, Brooks's hopes were dashed the next day when Wayne met with him and told him that the script was one of the funniest things he had ever read, but that he couldn't do the film because it was just "too dirty." He pointed out that his fans would accept pretty much anything of their hero, but they wouldn't stand for him being in a "blue" movie. He tried to cushion the blow by telling Brooks that, when the film was released, he'd be first in line to see it.

After the disappointment of not being able to cast his cowboy, Brooks decided to go for the alcoholic—which, he soon discovered, was probably not the wisest move. He reached out to veteran actor Gig Young, whose battle with the bottle had all but overtaken his acting career during the past few years.

Born Byron Elsworth Barr in 1913, Young's early appearances—as Byron Barr—included small roles in *Misbehaving Husbands* (1940) and in shorts such as *Here Comes the Cavalry* (1941). He was performing onstage in a play called *Pancho* when he was spotted by a talent scout from Warner Brothers. He was given a contract with Warners almost immediately, and he appeared under the name Byron Barr in such films as *Sergeant York* (1941), *The Man Who Came to Dinner*, and *The Male Animal* (both 1942). His first notable role came about that same year in *The Gay Sisters* as a character called "Gig Young." Preview cards praised the actor and Warners decreed that Byron Barr would now be billed as Gig Young, in part because there was another actor in Hollywood called Byron Barr, who is best known today for his appearance in Billy Wilder's film noir classic *Double Indemnity* (1944).

Young was hesitant about the name change at first, but he felt audiences would remember the new name, and there would be no confusion with any other actor called "Gig," because there were none. Under the new moniker, Young's roles got juicier in such films as Howard Hawks's *Air Force* (1943) and as Bette Davis's love interest in *Old Acquaintance* that same year.

Young served in the U.S. Coast Guard during World War II, and at the end of the conflict, he was cast in a supporting role in the Errol Flynn vehicle *Escape Me Never* (1947) and *The Woman in White* (1948), after which he left Warner Brothers because he wasn't pleased with his salary.

Young freelanced for a time, becoming popular as a second male lead in numerous features, many of which were high-profile parts, such as Porthos in *The Three Musketeers* (1948), supporting John Wayne in *Wake of the Red Witch* that same year, and appearing with Robert Cummings and Rosalind Russell in *Tell It to the Judge* (1949). His first leading role was in the film noir thriller *Hunt the Man Down* (1951), and he received considerable acclaim for portraying an alcoholic in *Come Fill the Cup* that year alongside James Cagney. For that role, he was nominated for a Golden Globe and an Academy Award.

Young portrayed another "tipsy" character in *Teacher's Pet* (1958), in which he starred with Clark Gable and Doris Day. At this point, his career went from strength to strength, with appearances on Broadway in *Under the Yum-Yum Tree* throughout 1960 and 1961 and a number of television appearances, eventually landing his own series *The Rogues* in the 1964–1965 TV season. It was during the filming of this series that Young's alcoholism began to come to the forefront and affect his career negatively. Yet, in an odd way, his personal problems seemed to also give his career a boost: he finally won the Best Supporting Actor Oscar for his performance as the alcoholic dance marathon emcee in *They Shoot Horses, Don't They?* in 1969.

Young had mentioned to movie columnist Louella Parsons in 1951 that some actors seemed to have bad luck after winning Oscars; of course, he said that after losing the Academy Award that year. After his win in 1969, though, bad luck seemed to become a self-fulfilling prophecy for him, and he began to lose roles because of his increasingly debilitating alcoholism.

Brooks decided to give Young a chance after seeing him in the Joe Bologna/Renee Taylor comedy *Lovers and Other Strangers* (1970), which had been nominated for three Academy Awards. Brooks felt that he would be perfect for the part of the Waco Kid because he had both comedy and drama in his résumé. Young's agent assured Brooks that his client had been on the wagon for more than a year and always showed up for work completely sober.

The first day of shooting *Blazing Saddles* arrived on March 6, 1973. The scene filmed that day was the meeting between Cleavon Little as the new sheriff and Young as the Waco Kid, who was hanging upside down from his bunk in the jail cell of the sheriff's office, attempting to recover from a hangover.

In the scene, Little walks over to him and asks, "Are we awake?" The Waco Kid groggily replies, "We're not sure. Are we black?"

At least, those were the lines in the script. According to Brooks, Young replied, "We're not sure. Are we bla . . . are we bla . . . are we BLA?"

Brooks turned to his assistant director, John C. Chulay, and noted that Young's performance seemed very "real." It suddenly became all too real: instead of finishing the line, Young threw up all over the set. Brooks immediately had Chulay call an ambulance.

It became obvious that, contrary to what Young's agent had said, his client was not a recovering alcoholic. The ambulance took him to a nearby hospital, and he was treated for alcohol withdrawal. He was far too ill to perform for the next several months, and he would have to be replaced.

For whatever reason, the filming had commenced on a Friday, and Brooks was desperate. He called his old friend Gene Wilder, who had costarred with Zero Mostel in *The Producers*, and, "through tears," asked him to step in and save the picture. According to Brooks, Wilder's response was "I don't know whether to laugh or cry, but I'll be on a plane tomorrow morning."

The next day, the studio was closed as it was a Saturday, but they opened up a few departments for Brooks and Wilder. An employee of the wardrobe department assisted Wilder with a costume; they then looked through props and Wilder found an acceptable pair of six-shooters. Later, they drove out to the Warner Brothers ranch, where the actor chose a horse to ride and a white cowboy hat to wear. Brooks informed him that he wasn't the sheriff, but rather the sheriff's buddy, so Wilder rejected the white hat in favor of a dark hat. According to Brooks, Wilder had become the Waco Kid by the end of the day.

Wilder began life as Jerome Silberman, born in 1933 in Milwaukee, Wisconsin. His father was a Russian-Jewish immigrant, a manufacturer and salesman of novelty items. Wilder first became interested in acting at the tender age of eight, when his mother, Jeanne, came down with rheumatic fever and the doctor told the boy to "try and make her laugh." He started taking acting lessons at age thirteen, eventually becoming involved with a local theater company, performing for the first time in front of an audience at age fifteen in a production of *Romeo and Juliet*.

Wilder studied communication and theater arts at the University of Iowa, and following his graduation in 1955, he was accepted at the Bristol Old Vic Theatre School in Bristol, England. Among other subjects, he studied fencing there and became the first freshman to win the All-School Fencing Championship. Seeking new worlds to conquer, he decided to study the Stanislavski method of acting and returned to the United States, where he enrolled at the Herbert Berghof Studio in Greenwich Village.

His acting training was interrupted by basic training when he was drafted into the U.S. Army in 1956, where he was assigned to the medical corps. When he was discharged from the army in 1958, he returned to New York with a scholarship to the Herbert Berghof Studio, allowing him to become a full-time student. He supported himself with odd jobs, including that of fencing instructor.

Wilder's first professional acting assignment was in a Herbert Berghof production of Shakespeare's *Twelfth Night* in Cambridge, Massachusetts, in which he also choreographed the fencing scenes. After studying for three years at the HB Studio, Wilder was accepted into the Actors Studio, which specialized in Lee Strasberg's Method acting technique. This was when he adopted his stage name, feeling that "Jerry Silberman" just didn't sound sophisticated enough. True to form, his stage name was chosen from theater and literature: he got the "Gene" from the character Eugene Grant in Thomas Wolfe's novel *Look Homeward*,

Angel, while "Wilder" was filched from Thornton Wilder, who wrote *Our Town*, among other great American plays.

Wilder performed in some off-Broadway shows such as Sir Arnold Wesker's *Roots* (not to be confused with Alex Haley's *Roots*) and Graham Greene's *The Complaisant Lover*; in 1963 through 1964, he received acclaim for playing mental patient Billy Bibbitt in the Broadway production of Ken Kesey's novel *One Flew Over the Cuckoo's Nest*, appearing with star Kirk Douglas.

Also in 1963, Wilder played a leading role in Bertold Brecht's play *Mother Courage and Her Children*, starring Anne Bancroft, who introduced him to her then-boyfriend and future husband Mel Brooks. Several months later, Brooks mentioned to Wilder that he was working on *Springtime for Hitler*, and that he thought Wilder would be great in the role of Leo Bloom. Brooks asked Wilder to check with him before he made any long-term theatrical plans.

Meanwhile, Wilder toured the country in various plays and appeared in a CBS-TV production of *Death of a Salesman* in 1966 as Bernard. His first appearance in a theatrical film was as hostage Eugene Grizzard in Arthur Penn's *Bonnie and Clyde* the following year. Finally, three years after Brooks had mentioned *Springtime for Hitler* to him, Wilder was asked to come in for a reading with Zero Mostel, who was to star in the film that eventually became known as *The Producers*. Mostel, as the star of the film, had to approve of his costar and, fortunately for Wilder, he did; as Brooks had promised, he was cast as Leo Bloom and the rest is cinematic history. It was worth the wait; he was nominated for an Academy Award for Best Supporting Actor in the role.

In 1969, Wilder went to Paris to perform a leading role in Bud Yorkin's *Start the Revolution without Me*, a wild comedy set during the

French Revolution, which costarred Donald Sutherland. After production ended on that film, Wilder returned to New York, where he read the script for *Quackser Fortune Has a Cousin in the Bronx*. Enchanted by Gabriel Walsh's screenplay, Wilder contacted Sidney Glazier, who had produced *The Producers*, and asked him if he could help him find a director for the project. Legendary French director Jean Renoir (*La Grande Illusion*, 1937) was their first choice, but he was tied up with projects for at least a year. Wilder and Glazier ultimately settled on British-Indian filmmaker Waris Hussein (*A Touch of Love*, 1969) to direct. Costarring with a young Margot Kidder, Wilder traveled to Dublin to film *Quackser Fortune* in August and September of 1969.

Two years later, Wilder read for the lead role in *Willy Wonka and the Chocolate Factory*, directed by Mel Stuart from Roald Dahl's book *Charlie and the Chocolate Factory*. Stuart offered him the role on the spot, which was quite a coup for the actor, as everyone from Fred Astaire to Spike Milligan to Peter Sellers was considered for the part of Willy Wonka.

Although *Willy Wonka and the Chocolate Factory* was not an immediate success, it received positive reviews and eventually became a much-beloved cult film. It also received an Oscar nomination for Best Musical Score (by Leslie Bricusse and Anthony Newley) and scored a Golden Globe nomination for Wilder as Best Actor.

At this point, Wilder's career was going along swimmingly, although none of his movies so far had been major hits at the box office. That all changed when Woody Allen offered him a role in a segment of his comedy anthology film *Everything You Always Wanted to Know about Sex * (*But Were Afraid to Ask)* in 1972. The movie was a great success, grossing a whopping (for the time) $18 million dollars in the United States, which was six times its production cost.

Wilder fleshed out the story of how he came to be cast in *Blazing Saddles* in his own autobiography, *Kiss Me Like a Stranger: My Search for Love and Art*. According to Wilder, Brooks called him from a pay phone and asked, "Can you come right away?"

Wilder informed Brooks that he was scheduled to be in London in two weeks to appear in *The Little Prince* for director Stanley Donen. Brooks begged Wilder to call Donen and tell him he could come to London at a later date.

Wilder wrote,

> I called Stanley in London and told him the situation. He said, "Do you really want to do Mel's film?" I said, "I really want to help Mel if I can." Stanley said, "All right—I'll shoot your scenes at the end of the schedule instead of at the beginning." I left for Los Angeles the next day.
>
> The following day, I was looking at Cleavon Little, who appeared to be upside down, since I was hanging upside down in a jail cell.
>
> "Are we black?" I asked.

Although some sources insist Wilder was asked to replace Dan Duryea in the role, Brooks and Wilder settled that controversy in their respective autobiographies: as we know now, he was asked to replace Gig Young. The confusion seems to stem from the fact that Duryea had once been under consideration for the role, but poor health and declining eyesight had forced him to turn down the offer.

Interestingly enough, most of *Blazing Saddles* was filmed in the same Old West outdoor sets—called Laramie Street, located in the back lot of Warner Brothers Studios—that were used for Michael Crichton's *Westworld* in the previous year. Other locations included Vasquez Rocks Natural Area Park in Aqua Dulce for most of the railroad scenes, the famed Grauman's Chinese Theater in Los Angeles for the wild finale, Beaudette and Mojave-Tropico Road in Rosamund for some additional railroad scenes and the fake town, buttes in Palmdale for additional second unit shots, the town of Santa Clarita, and stages 15 and 28 at Warner Brothers Burbank Studios.

Some scenes that ended up in the film came from Brooks's own experiences, or those of people he knew. The scene in which Little aims the gun at his own head to prevent the townsfolk from lynching him was inspired by an incident that happened to Brooks when he was a child. In his autobiography, he wrote that he stole a pack of gum and a water pistol from a drugstore. When one of the store employees accused him of stealing, he held the clerk at bay using the very water pistol he had just pilfered.

The scene in which Mongo knocks out a horse also has a basis in reality. According to Brooks, his former boss Sid Caesar—a physically imposing, moody, and sometimes violent man—told him that once when he was riding horses on a trail with his wife, her horse caused her some problems, and Caesar ended up punching it between the eyes. He claimed that the horse collapsed, unconscious. Whether it was true or not is irrelevant; it made for a very funny scene. In the film, of course, the horse was not injured but trained to fall on command.

Several scenes were shot but cut from the finished film. A sequence in which Bart tricks Mongo into diving for treasure was deleted, along with a scene with the governor (Brooks) and the press touring the phony Rock Ridge. The latter scene was edited back in for the network television broadcast years later, as so much of the more "offensive" scenes had to be censored for TV.

Speaking of "offensive," actress Hedy Lamarr was offended and sued Warner Brothers during production when she got wind of the fact that one of the characters was called "Hedley Lamarr." By that time, Lamarr was a *grand dame* of old Hollywood, having emigrated from her native Austria to the United States after the worldwide (and infamous) success of *Ecstasy* (1933), which featured several brief nude scenes of the actress and even a rare—for the time—sequence focusing on Lamarr's face as she is in the throes of orgasm. The film received an award at the Venice Film Festival and was considered something of an artistic triumph in Europe, but not so in Puritanical America, where it was banned. There's no such thing as bad publicity, however, and Lamarr found herself in demand for more films showcasing her considerable acting talents.

Lamarr met movie magnate Louis B. Mayer in London, where he signed her immediately to a contract with MGM. She became a star in MGM's *Algiers* (1938) and went on to continued success in such films as *White Cargo* (1942) and her biggest hit, *Samson and Delilah* (1949), in which she costarred with Victor Mature.

She was retired at the time of *Blazing Saddles'* production, and very protective of her public image and her privacy. Mind you, Hedy Lamarr was not even her real name—she was born Hedwig Eva Maria Kiesler— but in her $100,000 lawsuit against Warner Brothers, she claimed that the parodic use of the name "Hedley Lamarr" throughout *Blazing Saddles* infringed on her right to privacy. Brooks later said he was actually flattered by the lawsuit from the Hollywood legend, and that he decided not to fight it in court. Ultimately, the studio settled for a small sum and apologized for "almost using her name." Brooks said that Lamarr "never got the joke," but that didn't keep him from referencing the matter as an in-joke in the film, in which the governor (Brooks) tells Lamarr, "This is 1874. You'll be able to sue *her*."

The course of production itself went rather smoothly, although the salty language in the script gave some of the actors pause. Burton Gilliam, who played one of the villainous henchmen, didn't feel comfortable using the N-word on Sheriff Bart; he found Little to be a very likable guy, and he just didn't want to use racial slurs on him, finding it difficult to separate the actor from the character.

After doing several takes of the "offending" scene, Little took Gilliam aside, sensing his difficulty. He assured him that what he said was okay because those weren't really his words. Little went on to say, "If I thought you would say those words to me in any other situation, we'd go to fist city, but this is all fun. Don't worry about it."

Little got along great with Wilder, by all accounts; in fact, they became fast friends. As Little was mainly a stage actor, Wilder took him under his wing and gave him pointers about how to act in front of a camera. And one of the funniest lines in the film between their two characters was improvised.

Everyone who has seen *Blazing Saddles* knows this scene: Jim, a.k.a. the Waco Kid, is talking to Sheriff Bart about the people of Rock Ridge, and he seems to wax poetic when he goes into this bit: "You've got to remember that these are just simple farmers. These are people of the land. The common clay of the New West. You know . . . morons."

At that last line, Sheriff Bart cracks up. Little's reaction was genuine: Wilder ad-libbed "You know . . . morons." Brooks knew about it but didn't tip off Little. He wanted this to be real, to be playful. This moment remains one of the most enjoyable of the entire film, both because of the painstaking, straight-faced way in which Wilder delivers the lines and in Little's true, honest reaction to them.

Some cast members took the reality of this comedy seriously, as it were. Take Slim Pickens, for example. A veteran of more western movies than probably even he could remember, he was also a lifelong member of the National Rifle Association. For the desert scenes, Pickens stayed in his RV (recreational vehicle) and would sit out by a campfire in the evening, with his trusty Winchester rifle by his side. Some might call that Method acting; whatever it was, it was an example of how much the actors wanted to make *Blazing Saddles* something special.

Pickens features in one of the more, shall we say, memorable scenes in the film: when the cowboys are sitting around the campfire eating beans and proceed to pass wind, one after the other. Supposedly, *Blazing Saddles* was the movie that broke "the fart barrier." There had never been a scene like this before. According to Brooks, he and his coconspirators came up with this outlandish idea after watching countless old western films in which the cowboys seemed to consume only black coffee and an endless supply of beans. To Brooks, there could only be one outcome of this prairie feasting: farting. Allegedly, the sound effects for this infamous scene were added in the editing room by Brooks himself and anyone who happened to pass by. It's probably for the best that we don't know any more details than that.

You don't have to be a film buff to get all the jokes in *Blazing Saddles*, but if you know your classic movies, it certainly enhances the movie. Take Robert Ridgely's medieval hangman, known as Boris: he's actually a parody of Mord, the medieval executioner in the film *Tower of London* (1939)—who was played by Boris Karloff.

There are myriad in-jokes in the movie, including a nod to a more recent film, in fact one of Brooks's own. When Hedley's men ride through the fake Rock Ridge, there's a fast cut to Kahn as Lili Von Schtüpp singing a drinking song with a few German soldiers. They're singing the same song that Wilder, Zero Mostel, and Kenneth Mars were singing in *The Producers*. When we first see Von Schtüpp's poster, we hear the first four bars of "Springtime for Hitler" played on an old-time player piano.

The in-jokes run fast and furious throughout *Blazing Saddles*. For example, when Mongo rides into town, a Mexican can be heard shouting, "Mongo! Santa Maria!" Mongo Santamaria was a well-known Cuban jazz musician at the time. The bull that Mongo rides has the word YES painted on one side and NO on the other. This was apparently a reference to the fifties policy of marking the backs of school buses as to which side was safe for cars to pass. The implication here is that Mongo and his ox are as big as a bus.

The character of Governor Lepetomane was named after an early-twentieth-century French performer, Joseph Pujol, whose stage name was Lepetomane, a name that combined the French verb peter ("to fart") with mane ("maniac"); his stage name, therefore, translates to "The Fartomaniac." Pujol was famous—or infamous—for his ability to control his abdominal muscles, enabling him to inhale air into his rectum and expel it at will. His profession, if you can call it that, was referred to as "fartist," "flatulist," or, if you really want to get lofty about it, "farteur." Onstage, he told stories punctuated with his flatulence, demonstrating his ability to blow out candle flames from up to two feet away (with his back turned, of course), and he performed "La Mar-sellaise" and other popular tunes with, well, his abdominal muscles. Hard to believe that people paid to see him, but it brings a new meaning to the term "artsy-fartsy," doesn't it?

The Indian Chief (also played by Brooks) speaks Yiddish. The English translations of his dialogue are "Blacks!" "Don't be crazy!" "Let them go!," and "Have you ever seen in your life?" Brooks's Yiddish Indian Chief was essentially a parody of Chief Scar in *The Searchers* (1956), who was played by Henry Brandon, a German-born Jew.

The name of the character played by Dom DeLuise—Buddy Bizarre—is a takeoff on the famed dance choreographer Busby Berkeley, famed for his elaborate and perfectly timed routines in such films as *Dames* (1934), *Gold Diggers of 1937* (1936), and *Varsity Show* (1937). "The French Mistake," which Buddy Bizarre is choreographing toward the end of *Blazing Saddles*, is a parody of such routines. DeLuise later said that the role of Buddy Bizarre was originally intended for Peter Sellers. After Brooks endured a four-hour audition by Sellers—who was notoriously difficult to work with—he decided to cast his old friend DeLuise instead.

The breaking of the "fourth wall" at the film's riotous conclusion contains an ad-libbed moment of its own. When the whole group of actors are running out of the Warner Brothers gates, there's a man wearing a sweater standing on the sidewalk, watching the action. Brooks later said that the man was not supposed to have been in the shot but had merely stopped by to watch the action. When he first showed up, Brooks and his assistants told him to please stay out of the shot and, at first, he did. He couldn't resist coming back, however, and apparently didn't fully understand what he had been asked to do, so he just stood there. Ultimately, Brooks decided he could be in the shot and asked him to sign a waiver to appear in the film. And now the anonymous man in a sweater is immortalized in *Blazing Saddles*.

A large photo of actor Edward G. Robinson can be seen hanging on the wall of the commissary during the pie fight. Toward the conclusion of the final fight scene, the camera pans across the Warner Brothers Studios buildings, and sharp-eyed viewers will spot another set near the back. This is the set that served as the southern town in the late seventies–early eighties TV series *The Dukes of Hazzard*. Fans of that show will instantly recognize the town hall and police station from that series.

Brooks is literally all over the film, although he ended up cutting many of his scenes as Lepetomane because he felt it slowed the picture down. Yet his numerous on-screen cameos such as the Indian Chief and an anonymous aviator ultimately extended to include voice-overs. For example, the voice of the drunk who Lili Von Shtüpp kicks off the stage is provided by Brooks, as was the voice of the German soldier who joins her later in the scene.

The snack "Raisinets" are mentioned in one scene, and Brooks said he received packages of Raisinets from the company for years as a kind of "thank you." He never received such gratitude from the Howard Johnson company; the Howard Johnson's Ice Cream Parlor that's seen in the town of Rock Ridge was an in-jokey reference to the Howard Johnson's restaurant and hotel chain, which was known at the time for its "28 flavors" of ice cream. Sheriff Bart's reference to "the orange roof on Howard Johnson's outhouse" was a poke at the restaurants, known for their orange roofs. The chain was at its peak in the seventies, with over a thousand restaurants and hotels throughout the United

States. Sadly, by 2021 there was only one restaurant left, located in Lake George, New York. That location finally closed in 2022, so there are no more Howard Johnson's restaurants, although a few hotels are still scattered here and there. And they're immortalized, of course, in *Blazing Saddles*.

Some of the pop culture references in *Blazing Saddles* are pretty obscure. At the opening of the scene in which Mongo awakens in the sheriff's office, Bart is hanging up "wanted" posters on the board. There's one "wanted" poster already hanging there, and eagle-eyed viewers with some knowledge of western movies may recognize it as the same poster seen on the wall in the jail house in the classic Howard Hawks/John Wayne western *Rio Bravo* (1959). And for those inveterate TV watchers, there's a flashback scene involving young Bart riding in a covered wagon along with his family; young Bart was played by Rodney Allen Rippy, well known at the time for his national commercials for Jack-in-the-Box hamburgers.

The character of Van Johnson (Furth) always wears red socks in the film; the rather esoteric reason for this is because Furth claimed that he had heard that the actor Van Johnson always wore red socks. There's no reason given for Megowan's on-screen credit as "Gum Chewer"; however, he does, in fact, play another role in the movie: he's the drunk who Von Shtüpp pushes into the audience after he totters toward her onstage.

When he hands out the paddle balls to his cohorts at the table, Lepetomane calls each of them by name as Frankie, Johnny, Patsy, and Kelly; "Frankie and Johnny" was a popular song in the thirties when Brooks was a kid, and "Patsy" may have been a reference to Patsy Kelly, a well-known comic actress during that same decade.

Mongo, the character created by Pryor, was most likely based on the character "Nitro Rankin" as played by Guinn "Big Boy" Williams in Charles Vidor's western *The Desperados* (1943). Both Williams and Karras, as it happens, were professional sportsmen, although Williams was in baseball rather than football.

The in-jokes in *Blazing Saddles* extend to the music. Brooks is a huge fan of popular songs, despite the fact that he can't read music. Nevertheless, it's been an important part of his films, going all the way back to *The Producers*. He composed the song "Springtime for Hitler" for that film by humming the tune into a tape recorder, then had it transcribed by someone who had musical knowledge. This became the way he composed all his songs, including the ones in *Blazing Saddles*, as we shall see in the next chapter.

5

SINGING THEIR WAY INTO YOUR HEART

Brooks wrote the lyrics for the *Blazing Saddles* theme song, which were typically Brooksian. Although, at first glance, the lyrics involving a sheriff and his shiny badge seemed serious enough, when one read between the lines, there was no way that a "blazing saddle" didn't have a double meaning.

But who to sing the song? Brooks had some very definite ideas about that. He had in mind a "Frankie Laine" type. Laine was a Chicago-born singer, composer, and author who had worked with such musical luminaries as Hoagy Carmichael and Nat King Cole. His song hits included "That's My Desire," "Mule Train," and "On the Sunny Side of the Street," but, more to the point, Brooks wanted a "Frankie Laine" type because of his warbling the title tunes for such western classics as *3:10 to Yuma, Gunfight at the O.K. Corral* (both 1957), and the theme for the TV western *Rawhide* beginning in 1959, the series that introduced Clint Eastwood into the public consciousness.

According to his autobiography, Brooks said to himself, "If we want a Frankie Laine type, why not get Frankie himself?" Two days after a classified ad for a "Frankie Laine" type ran in the LA newspapers, Laine himself showed up at Brooks's office, ready for work. Brooks didn't tell Laine the movie was a parody of the western genre, and he just advised Laine to let 'er rip with the song, on which Brooks had collaborated with composer John Morris. Brooks later wrote, "To my amazement, after he finished a beautiful heart-rending rendition of 'Blazing Saddles,' he told me, 'I really love that song.'"

After scoring *The Producers*, John Morris became Brooks's go-to composer. Born in Elizabeth, New Jersey, in 1926, Morris had studied at Julliard School and composed incidental music and dance numbers for several Broadway productions, including *Baker Street* (1963), *Dear World* (1969), and many others, and wrote and produced his own musical in 1966 called *A Time for Singing*. Prior to *The Producers*, Brooks had worked with Morris on two stage musicals, *Shinbone Alley* (1957) and *All-American* (1962). Morris did the original arrangement for "Springtime for Hitler" in *The Producers* and composed the entire film score. He went on to score *The Twelve Chairs* for Brooks.

By the time Morris scored *Blazing Saddles*, he and Brooks had a "shorthand," as Brooks wrote in his memoirs: "I wrote 'I'm Tired' for Lili von Shtüpp and he orchestrated it in single instruments like they did in Berlin in 1920. I thought I'd hear it in a normal orchestration, but he got the incredible Berliner Ensemble feeling like Bertolt Brecht and Kurt Weill's *The Threepenny Opera*. It was just amazing."

Brooks noted, "'I'm Tired' was the dirtiest song I ever wrote." The lyrics concerned Von Shtüpp's, um, "career" involving thousands of men. Her world-weary "tiredness" is the point of the tune. Kahn turned out to be the perfect choice to sing it, as Brooks discovered when they set about filming it.

Brooks later wrote of the scene,

> The most fun was shooting the Lili von Shtüpp saloon number.
> . . . I took special care to write lyrics that would blend with our
> Dietrich-esque Lili von Shtüpp's slightly off-key notes. "I'm
> Tired" is a salute to world-weary women everywhere, who give
> in to the inability of men to make love properly. Madeline
> loved it, and her performance was absolutely out of this world.
> We were lucky to get Alan Johnson, who had choreographed
> "Springtime for Hitler," to do the crazy Teutonic dance steps
> for us. I was hoping the audience would agree with me after
> they saw pointy-helmeted Germans singing and dancing in a
> western saloon—that this picture was downright crazy!

"I'm Tired" is actually a parodic homage to Dietrich's performance of Cole Porter's song "I'm the Laziest Gal in Town" in Alfred Hitchcock's *Stage Fright* (1950), with a bit of Friedrich Hollaender "Falling in Love Again (Can't Help It)" thrown in, the latter of which Dietrich performed in Josef von Sternberg's *The Blue Angel* (1930). Brooks's knowledge of film history certainly served him well in the writing and production of *Blazing Saddles*.

Brooks wrote the music and lyrics for "The Ballad of Rock Ridge," sung by a chorus in the film. The lyrics again were typically Brooksian, beginning slowly and seriously, gradually building up into a punchline that involved the word "shit."

The final original song in *Blazing Saddles* is "The French Mistake," in which DeLuise (as Buddy Bizarre) is attempting to direct a chorus of—shall we say—rather effeminate men dressed in top hats, white ties, and tails in a singing and dancing routine just before the big pie fight. Again written by Brooks, some of the lyrics were a tad suggestive, all done in a late 1920s/early 1930s musical style that includes just about every gay stereotype one can imagine.

Not all the songs in *Blazing Saddles* are original, however. The film actually begins with a chorus of railroad workers singing "Swing Low, Sweet Chariot," the classic spiritual written by Wallace Willis, which morphs into Cole Porter's "I Get a Kick Out of You." Later on, portions of "April in Paris" by Vernon Duke and E. Y. Harburg are performed out in the desert by Count Basie and His Orchestra, a surreal moment if ever there was one. The arrangement that Basie presides over in the film was made by him in 1955 and was recorded by him twice, first as an instrumental and again as a vocal with Ella Fitzgerald at the 1956 Newport Jazz Festival.

More surrealism ensues when "Merrily We Roll Along," the title theme to the Warner Brothers *Merrie Melodies* cartoons, pops into the movie out of nowhere. Written by Charlie Tobias, Murray Mencher, and Eddie Cantor, "Merrily We Roll Along" is an iconic tune and one that Brooks insisted on putting into *Blazing Saddles* to accent its craziness and sense of anarchy.

Music has always been an integral part of Brooks's films. There was even a record album of "greatest hits" from his movies released in 1978 called *The Mel Brooks Songbook*, which featured "Blazing Saddles," "I'm Tired," and "The French Mistake," along with songs that Brooks and Morris composed for *The Producers*, *The Twelve Chairs*, *Silent Movie* (1976), and *High Anxiety* (1977). Morris became a hugely important member of Brooks's unofficial "stock company," ultimately composing scores for twenty of Brooks's films, including the non-comedy movies made under the Brooksfilms banner, the company that Brooks formed in 1980 to produce more "serious" films. Morris's scores for Brooksfilms included such highly regarded works as *The Elephant Man* (1980), for which the composer garnered an Oscar nomination. Morris died in 2018 at the ripe old age of ninety-one, but his music lives on.

6

RIDING TALL IN THE SADDLE

Brooks's best friend on *Blazing Saddles* turned out to be John Calley, Warner Bros. studio executive and producer. In 1973, Calley was president of Warner Bros. under studio head Frank Wells. Unlike Wells, Calley was a forward thinker with an open mind. With postproduction on *Blazing Saddles* completed in January 1974, Brooks arranged a screening for the studio executives. It was a disaster. As Brooks said years later, "When we screened it for executives, there were few laughs. The head of distribution said, 'Let's dump it and take a loss.'"

Brooks subsequently set up a screening for studio employees and the public at the Avco Embassy Theater on Wilshire Boulevard in Los Angeles. As Brooks is nothing if not a showman, he had the lobby filled with live cattle, "mooing and doing what live cattle do." Perhaps the atmosphere helped, because every seat was sold out and, as Brooks wrote, "The audience loved it—they went bananas!" He continued: "To work so hard on a film for so long and to be rewarded with nonstop riotous laughter is the greatest payment in the world. It was an incredible screening . . . as they say in *Variety*, 'A LAFF RIOT!'"

There was one slight problem, however: on the way out of the screening, Wells took Brooks aside into the manager's office, where Brooks got Calley to come along "for moral support." Wells handed Brooks a legal pad and pencil and instructed him to take notes. He wanted several scenes and many instances of dialogue removed from the film: the flatulence scene, the scene in which Karras punches the horse, the N-word throughout, the risqué scenes with the secretary, the song "I'm Tired"; all of these things were to be taken out. Brooks duly jotted down all the notes. The moment that Wells left the office, Brooks threw all the notes into the wastepaper basket. "Well filed," said Calley.

Brooks was already good at playing the Hollywood game, but, after being backed up by Calley, he felt secure in not following any of the Warner Bros. "suggestions." He and Calley both knew that it would end up being "the shortest film in history" were he to do what Wells wanted. Brooks never cut a single scene, save for one tiny line: in the scene in which Lili and Bart are alone in the darkened room, Lili excitedly shouts, "It's twue! It's twue!" In the original version, Bart quietly says, "I hate to disappoint you, ma'am, but you're sucking on my arm." Brooks cut that one line (it was later restored when the movie was released to video).

More than one Warners executive had been concerned about the frequent use of the N-word, but Brooks received constant support in that department from both Little and Pryor, and more recently, Brooks has said that if the film were remade today, use of that word would indeed be objectionable "and then, you have no movie." As Wilder said of the film and its makers, "They've smashed racism in the face, but they're doing it while you laugh."

Blazing Saddles officially premiered on February 7, 1974, at the Pickwick Drive-In Theater in Burbank, California. It was attended by 250 invited guests, with Little and Wilder riding horses to the event and watching the film on horseback. Again, the screening was a smash success, and Calley insisted that the film open in stages across the country, starting in New York City, Chicago, and Los Angeles. It quickly went on to become the studio's top moneymaker throughout the spring and summer of 1974.

Not all the critics got the joke. Under the headline "*Blazing Saddles*, a Western in Burlesque," *New York Times* critic Vincent Canby wrote, "Some film comedies, like Jacques Tati's *Playtime* and Woody Allen's *Sleeper* stay with you after you've seen them. The humor, firmly rooted in the wilder contradictions of life, flourishes in the memory. Other comedies, like Mel Brooks's *Blazing Saddles*, the best title of the year to date, are like Chinese food. A couple of hours later, you wonder where it went."

Canby went on to write, "The trouble is that *Blazing Saddles* has no center of gravity . . . *Blazing Saddles* has no dominant personality, and it looks as if it includes every gag thought up in every story conference. Whether good, bad or mild, nothing was thrown out."

Gary Arnold of the *Washington Post* was even more negative; under the headline "*Blazing Saddles* on a Dead Horse," he wrote, "Mel Brooks squanders a snappy title on a stockpile of stale jokes. To say that this slapdash western spoof lacks freshness and spontaneity and originality is putting it mildly. *Blazing Saddles* is at once a messy and antiquated gag machine." *New York Magazine* critic John Simon also missed the point when he wrote, "All kinds of gags—chiefly anachronisms, irrelevancies, reverse ethnic jokes, and out and out vulgarities—are thrown together pell-mell, batted about insanely in all directions, and usually beaten into the ground."

Those critics who did get the jokes tended to be the less snooty and more down-to-earth types, such as Roger Ebert (who won a Pulitzer Prize for making his film reviews accessible to the "common clay," as it were) writing in the *Chicago Sun-Times*,

> There are some people who can get away with anything—say anything, do anything—and people will let them. Other people attempt a mildly dirty joke and bring total silence down on a party. Mel Brooks is not only a member of the first group, he is its lifetime president. At its best, his comedy operates in areas so far removed from taste that (to coin his own expression) it rises below vulgarity.
>
> *Blazing Saddles* is like that. It's a crazed grab-bag of a movie that does everything to keep us laughing except hit us over the head with a rubber chicken. Mostly, it succeeds. . . . It's an audience picture; it doesn't have a lot of classy polish and its structure is a total mess. But of course! What does that matter when Alex Karras is knocking a horse cold with a right cross to the jaw?

His compatriot over at the *Chicago Tribune*, Gene Siskel, also got the joke. Under the headline "Shootout at Cockeyed Corral," he enthused, "Bound to be one of the funniest of the year. . . . Whenever the laughs begin to run dry, Brooks and his quartet of gag writers splash about in a pool of obscenities that score belly laughs if your ears aren't sensitive and if you're hip to western movie conventions being parodied."

Even the ordinarily snooty *Monthly Film Bulletin* appreciated the film's bawdy humor, where Jan Dawson wrote, "Perhaps it is pedantic to point out that the whole is not equal to the sum of its parts when, for the curate's egg that it is, *Blazing Saddles* contains so many good parts and memorable performances." Under the headline "Was the West Ever Like this?," *Los Angeles Times* critic Charles Champlin opined, "*Blazing Saddles* is . . . irreverent, outrageous, improbable, often as blithely tasteless as a stag night at the Friar's Club and almost continuously funny." And the Bible of the entertainment industry, *Variety*, summed it up nicely in one of their film review sections for the February 13, 1974, edition: "If comedies are measured by the number of yocks they generate from audiences, then *Blazing Saddles* must be counted a success."

Whether the critics were yay or nay on the film was probably irrelevant: audiences flocked to it in droves, in spite of (or because of) the R rating, making it one of the biggest successes for Warner Bros. for that year. *Blazing Saddles* made $26.7 million during its initial release, a hefty sum for those days. It was reissued only two years later to earn over $10 million more, and again in 1979 when it brought in another $8 million for the studio. It ultimately grossed $119.5 million, making it one of only ten films up to that time to surpass the $100 million mark.

Despite its vulgarity and some negative criticism, *Blazing Saddles* received three Oscar nominations at the 47th Academy Awards: Best Film Editing by John C. Howard and Danford B. Greene; Best Song ("Blazing Saddles"), music by John Morris and lyrics by Mel Brooks; and Best Supporting Actress for Madeline Kahn. Although it didn't actually win any Oscars (they went to, respectively, Harold F. Kress and Karl Kress for *The Towering Inferno*; "We May Never Love Again Like

This" by Al Kasha and Joel Hirschhorn for the same movie; and Ingrid Bergman for *Murder on the Orient Express*), it was, as the saying goes, an honor just to be nominated, especially for such a wild comedy.

There was even an ill-fated television spin-off called *Black Bart*, starring Louis Gossett Jr. in the title role, with Steve Landesberg as his sidekick, a constantly drunken Confederate officer called Reb Jordan. Andrew Bergman was credited as the sole creator, and the pilot film was broadcast on April 4, 1975. The supporting cast included Gerrit Graham, a young Brooke Adams, and Noble Willingham, but *Black Bart* was doomed to failure because of the television restrictions of the time. As it was broadcast on CBS, network censorship meant that the bawdy humor of the film would have to be toned down for the proposed TV series, which meant that *Black Bart* would have none of the manic, risqué, and downright vulgar appeal of its progenitor.

The only reason that *Black Bart* came about at all was because, when the film was released and it was obviously going to be a big success, Brooks was aware that Warner Bros. would want a sequel or spin-off, whether or not he was personally involved. Brooks didn't like the sound of that and met with his attorneys to put a clause into the contract that a sequel would never be produced. During a 2005 university tour, Brooks explained,

> My lawyers, bless their souls, came to me and said, "Warner Bros. is going to try and take control of the movie. Let's put in a crazy condition that says they can't do any sequels unless they make it right away or make a TV show of it within six months." Which is brilliant. They couldn't make a sequel in six months and the movie was too vulgar to be a TV show. Now it

would air in family hour if that was still a thing. So the lawyers put that in never thinking they'd make it a TV show.

Brooks walked away from the situation, secure in his belief that a *Blazing Saddles* sequel or spin-off—neither of which he wanted anything to do with—would never be produced. Yet only a year later, CBS aired a "comedy special" called *Black Bart*. *TV Guide* for April 4, 1975, listed it as follows: "'Black Bart' is a hip black sheriff appointed to uphold the law in a rough and tumble Wild West town. In this series pilot based on *Blazing Saddles*, Bart overcomes hostility with cunning in obtaining a beautiful but expensive new gun, and in bringing the mayor's nephew to justice for toe-shooting."

Produced by CBS, with Warner Bros. offering the network sole rights to any and all potential *Blazing Saddles* films in exchange for production, the pilot was completed quickly. Warner Bros. knew a goldmine when they saw one, and they weren't about to let Brooks's nonparticipation be an issue. *Black Bart* was filmed during the winter break, a time during which most TV series were on hiatus. Brooks wasn't even aware of the production at the time.

The intention was to produce six episodes of the half-hour sitcom per season—as opposed to the twenty-six or twenty-nine episodes of most sitcoms of the time—to be broadcast on CBS. At one time, the rumor was that the series had actually been produced between 1974 and 1979 but had never been aired. It ultimately was revealed that no episodes of the series beyond the pilot had ever been filmed. The pilot was later included as a bonus feature on the thirtieth anniversary Blu-ray release of *Blazing Saddles*.

Black Bart is an unexceptional seventies sitcom, complete with canned laugh track, that does very little with its premise. Originally, the pilot was written by Michael Elias and Frank Shaw. Elias was a comedy veteran, having written for such series as *The Bill Cosby Show*, *All in the Family*, and *The Odd Couple*. Shaw had a similar background and had written for many of the same series. Together, they wrote a pilot called *Superdude*, in which the leading character was called Johnny Digs. When Bergman was asked by Warner Bros. to "create" *Black Bart* for television, he rewrote the script and turned it into the pilot for the proposed series.

Originally, three actors were in line for the role of Black Bart: Gossett, Richard Pryor, and of course Cleavon Little. At the time, Gossett was a busy television actor, appearing in episodes of such series as *The Partridge Family*, *Bonanza*, and *Mod Squad*. Pryor and Little were busy with other projects, so Gossett ended up getting the part.

The role of Belle, the town prostitute, was offered to Sally Kellerman, Tammy Grimes, and Amanda Blake, all of whom either turned it down or were unavailable. It ended up going to Millie Slavin, another TV veteran who had appeared in episodes of *The Bob Newhart Show*, *Rhoda*, and *The Rockford Files*, among many other shows. Bert Remsen, Lou Frizzell, and Sorrell Booke were all considered for the role of Fern Malaga, but for whatever reason, the part went to Willingham.

Gossett does what he can with the role, and in fact is quite engaging. Unfortunately, the writing just isn't there. Brooks's nonparticipation in the pilot is painfully apparent: for one thing, none of the (already) beloved characters from *Blazing Saddles* are in the pilot, aside from Black Bart himself. That's because the other characters for the film had been created by Brooks, Pryor, and Steinberg, and, as none of those writers were involved with the pilot, the characters they created couldn't legally appear in it. There's no Waco Kid, although Landesberg's character is obviously based on that character. Sadly, it's such a poorly written role that the actor can never gain any traction with it. Landesberg was a skilled comic actor, as he would prove on such series as *Barney Miller*, but all we know about Reb is that he's a drunk with a somewhat tragic past. And the lines he's given just aren't funny.

Belle is a poor replacement for Lili von Shtüpp; let's face it, Madeline Kahn was irreplaceable in any role. And the rest of the characters are mostly bland and unmemorable. The N-word is used a couple of times—pretty much unthinkable in a TV sitcom today—but played for laughs then as an attempt to recapture some of the earthiness and downright rudeness of the film. Needless to say, it falls flat; and Bart is reduced to calling the mayor "Milkface" in retaliation.

At one point, Belle calls Malaga "schweinhund," to which he responds, "Oh, Belle, you're so sexy when you talk French!" There's a mildly amusing exchange between Belle and Bart when Belle comes on to him and asks, "You've got a white horse. Why can't you have a white girlfriend?" He responds, "Do you remember when those four dudes tied me up and threw me in the well?" "Ja," says Belle. "That was for having a white horse," Bart tells her.

The funniest line occurs late in the show, when Bart has Curley (Gerrit Graham) and his men surrounded. He calls out to Curley, "Give up, Curley, you're trapped! Drop your guns and tie each other up!" That's one of the very few lines that has any of the anarchic silliness of the movie, but it's far too little, too late.

If *Black Bart* were made today, say for a streaming channel, the only thing the producers would have to worry about would be the use of the N-word. Otherwise, they could pretty much be as raucous as they wanted (although "rape jokes" wouldn't be tolerated either). In the seventies, however, despite the fact that television censorship was loosening up considerably, there were still standards and practices—as TV censorship was called—and lines that television broadcasts could not cross without running afoul of the Federal Communications Commission (FCC). As a result, *Black Bart* seemed no more adventurous at the time than *The Brady Bunch*, and it has been—quite rightly—assigned to the dustbin of history.

But how does the genuine article—the one, the only, the original *Blazing Saddles*—hold up in the politically correct atmosphere of the twenty-first century? Let's take a closer look.

In 2000, The American Film Institute's list of "100 Years . . . 100 Laughs" listed *Blazing Saddles* as the sixth funniest film of all time, behind *Some Like It Hot* (1959), *Tootsie* (1982), *Dr. Strangelove* (1964), *Annie Hall* (1977), and *Duck Soup* (1933). Brooks may quibble with this list—he's gone on record as saying he thinks he made the funniest film of all time—but it's no small potatoes to be just behind Billy Wilder, Sydney Pollack, Stanley Kubrick, Woody Allen, and the Marx Brothers. One of the criteria for the list was "Laughs that echo across time, enriching America's film heritage and inspiring artists and audiences today."

When the thirtieth anniversary DVD of *Blazing Saddles* was released in 2004, Michael Ventre of NBC's *Today* show noted that the film "skewers just about every aspect of racial prejudice while keeping the laughs coming. It is this daring combination, and not just a series of wickedly funny gags, that makes *Blazing Saddles* worthy of a 30th anniversary celebration." Ventre went on to say, "Comedies that stand up over 30 years are extremely rare. *Blazing Saddles* is at the top of that very short list."

In 2006, *Blazing Saddles* was deemed "respectable"—well, almost—when it was pronounced "culturally, historically or aesthetically significant" by the Library of Congress and selected for preservation in the National Film Registry. *Blazing Saddles* has been called many things over the years, but up to that point, "culturally, historically or aesthetically significant" was not one of them.

By the time the fortieth anniversary rolled around in 2014, the movie was again given kudos, this time by Nadya Faulx at NPR (National Public Radio) with a slightly different slant. Faulx's piece, titled "*Blazing Saddles*, The Best Interracial Buddy Comedy, turns 40," began this way: "Mel Brooks's western spoof *Blazing Saddles* turns 40 Friday, and along with its over-the-top jabs at racism and Hollywood, it set the gold standard for what is now an overused cinema trope: the interracial buddy comedy."

Faulx continued: "In his tepid *New York Times* review, Vincent Canby called the film 'every western you've ever seen turned upside down and inside out.' But the real heart of the movie—the 'center of gravity' that Canby lamented was missing from the story—is the relationship between Bart and Jim."

Faulx brought her own fresh observations and interpretations to the film. After comparing it to various eighties "interracial buddy comedies" such as *Trading Places*, *48 Hours*, and *Beverly Hills Cop*, she points out, "Until Hollywood can offer a new, more realistic take on racial relationships, you're better off watching *Blazing Saddles*." She also notes that Wilder paired with Richard Pryor for the films *Silver Streak* (1976) and *Stir Crazy* (1980) as part of the slew of similarly themed comedies produced in the wake of *Blazing Saddles.*

In her assessment of *Blazing Saddles* as the first and best of these types of interracial buddy comedies (after the more dramatic approaches of *The Defiant Ones* in 1958 and *In the Heat of the Night* in 1967), Faulx writes of Brooks's movie, "So, it's on the table: Jim is white and Black Bart is, well, black. There's no tension to overcome, no soul-searching or come-to-Jesus/Kumbaya moment. Bart and Jim are never pitted against each other; they're allies right off the bat, and the enemy, in this case, is white racism."

Continuing her thoughtful reevaluation of the film, Faulx finds that not all of it dates well: "It is worth noting that as groundbreaking as *Blazing Saddles* was in terms of race, the same can't be said for its treatment of gays and women. The F-word—not *that* one—is thrown around liberally, and the four or so women who have lines in the film are either clutching their pearls or taking off their clothes. The movie isn't self-aware at all when it comes to certain groups."

All in all, Faulx's take on the movie is very fair, and a movie that was then forty years old couldn't realistically be expected to reflect the mores of 2014. Of course, all movies are products of their time, and the free-wheeling seventies are a far cry from the more reined-in twenty-first century. Times have changed and society is more sensitive to the lesbian, gay, bisexual, transgender, and queer/questioning (LGBTQ) community, to women, and to other "certain groups," as Faulx puts it. She writes, "No ethnic or racial stereotype goes unmentioned: Mexican *bandidos,* Chinese laborers in straw cone hats, Arabs of ambiguous origin riding on camels, and yes, a Jewish Native American, all make cameos in Brooks's bizarre world, but they're not the butt of the joke." She quotes Michael Green, senior lecturer of film and media studies at Arizona State University, who points out, "*Blazing Saddles* is a satire of racism; that's what makes it groundbreaking. [Brooks] . . . shows how stupid it is."

Faulx gets the joke when she writes, "Brooks has never been known for his subtlety, and *Blazing Saddles* is no exception. Gone are the earnest, long-winded speeches about racial harmony that characterized movies like *The Defiant Ones*; instead, the film, co-written by Richard Pryor, tackles race and racism head-on and with humor. (It's so un-PC that Brooks told Jimmy Kimmel in 2012 he wouldn't be able to make the film today.)"

It's worth pointing out that Faulx is a young journalist who wasn't yet born when *Blazing Saddles* was released in 1974, so she's looking at the film with a fresh eye. Of course, she wrote her piece on it in 2014, which was a couple of years before the whole "woke" movement took off. That term originated in African American vernacular English to describe those who are "alert to racial prejudice and discrimination." It soon came to be associated with being more generally aware of social inequities and is now used by the American left to describe ideas involving social justice and identity politics, including the notions of white privilege and slavery reparations, as well as sexism and discrimination against LGBTQ individuals. It's also, not incidentally, used now as a pejorative by the right wing against those they perceive as "too liberal" or "too far left."

In 2009, Brooks received a Kennedy Center Honors recognition, an annual honor given to those in the performing arts for their various contributions to American culture. The 2009 awards were given, as they always are, at the Kennedy Center Opera House in Washington,

DC. During his speech honoring Brooks, President Barack Obama mentioned that he went to see *Blazing Saddles* when he was twelve years old. When Brooks asked how he got in to see an R-rated film, Obama joked, "I think I had a fake I.D., that I got with my fake birth certificate." He then added, grinning, "The statute of limitations has passed."

The movie that Brooks once said was written out of anger at "white corruption, racism and Bible-thumping bigotry" had become respectable after all. Its long-lasting appeal stems, to a certain extent, from its instant acceptance by the moviegoing public. The American movie release schedule was less concerned with blockbuster openings in those days, and the major big-budget releases were not necessarily scheduled for summer or Christmas release in 1974. It was nevertheless a big surprise to everyone involved that *Blazing Saddles* became a monster "sleeper" hit that February. Even then, there was a general feeling in the industry that films released in February, April, or October were those in which the major studios had only limited confidence. That was certainly the case with Warner Bros. and *Blazing Saddles*. Their only hope was for returns that exceeded expectations, which they certainly received with Brooks's movie. It was the last film to be released in the dreary month of February to end up being the number one box-office draw of the year until Marvel's *Black Panther* in 2018. *Blazing Saddles* struck a nerve in 1974; it hit the cultural zeitgeist at just the right moment.

In September 2016, President Obama again honored Brooks, this time with the National Medal of the Arts and Humanities. Obama's sly sense of humor again caused Brooks to smile when he joked, "We are here today to honor the very best of their fields, creators who give every piece of themselves to their craft. As Mel Brooks once said to his writers on *Blazing Saddles*, which is a great film, 'Write anything you want, because we'll never be heard from again. We will all be arrested for this movie.'"

In 2017, Brooks presented a special screening of the film in a presentation of the film called *Mel Brooks: Back in the Saddle Again*, then touring in California. When interviewed by journalist Kelli Skye Fadroski at the Q&A after the screening, Brooks commented that he "still got goosebumps" when showing the film to an audience. He was ninety years old at the time.

The N-word is uttered thirteen times in *Blazing Saddles*. Compare that to 110 uses of it in Quentin Tarantino's *Django Unchained* (2012)—which was controversial—and Brooks's movie seems almost restrained. How did Tarantino get away with it? *Django Unchained* was about a freed slave, for one thing, and Tarantino argued that if he didn't use that word, it would have been dishonest for the period he was trying to depict; for another, it was a dramatic film, not comedic. Using the N-word for comic effect is frowned upon these days; it was actually frowned upon in 1974, but Brooks didn't care as he was making his own point about racism.

From the get-go, *Blazing Saddles* shows us we're in for something special. The Warner Bros. logo appears over a black screen and quickly burns away in a parody of the opening to the TV series *Bonanza* (1959–1973), which leads us directly into the opening credits, over which Laine sings the theme song. The credits look—and feel, thanks to the music—very much like those in a western from the 1950s.

The opening scene, in which the railroad workers choose to sing "I Get a Kick Out of You" rather than the expected "Swing Low, Sweet Chariot," gives us an idea of the anarchy we're in for. When Lyle (Burton) rides up, the workers (including Bart) are all working pretty quietly. Lyle admonishes them: "Now, come on, boys! Where's your spirit? I don't hear no singin'. When you was slaves, you sang like birds. Go on, how 'bout a good ol' [n----r] work song?"

Sophisticated urbanite that he is, Bart leads the chorus with "I Get a Kick Out of You." Lyle is incensed: "Hold it, hold it, hold it! What the hell is that shit? I meant a song. A real song, something like . . . " Lyle goes into "Swing Low, Sweet Chariot." The workers look more confused than anything else. "Don't know that one, huh?" Lyle asks them.

When Taggart (Pickens) shows up and hears the workers singing Cole Porter, he is not amused: "What in the wide, wide world of sports is goin' on here? I hired you people to get a bit of track laid, not to jump around like a bunch of Kansas City f----ts!" This line is a pretty good indication of how politically incorrect the rest of the film is going to be.

Later, Bart and his friend Charlie (Charles McGregor) manage to escape their railroad bondage with the aid of a handcart. Unfortunately for them, they end up sinking in quicksand. Taggart spots them struggling and comes up with the following *bon mot*: "Well, boys, the break's over. Don't just lay there gettin' a suntan. It ain't gonna do you no good no how."

A word about Pickens as Taggart: there is not one scene in which he features in which he is not funny. Taggart is a dimwit, no question, but it's more than that that makes him relentlessly hilarious. It's just a joy to see Pickens poking fun at his own screen persona, in which he played second fiddle to so many great western stars, from Errol Flynn to John Wayne. He was sometimes the comedy relief in those films, but more often he was a henchman, a bank robber, or a soldier. His comic delivery in *Blazing Saddles* is second to none and, like a horse thief, he steals many of his scenes. His chemistry with Korman is priceless.

At one point in the proceedings, Korman muses aloud, "My mind is a raging torrent, flooded with rivulets of thought cascading into a waterfall of creative alternatives." Taggart looks slightly puzzled, then responds, "God darn it, Mr. Lamarr, you use your tongue prettier than a twenty-dollar whore."

In another scene, Taggart attempts to help Lamarr in his quest to run people out of town. "I got it," he tells Lamarr. "I know how we can run everyone out of Rock Ridge." "How?" asks Lamarr. "We'll kill the first-born male child in every household." Lamarr looks thoughtful for a moment, then responds, "Too Jewish."

Later, Lamarr's posse, with Taggart in the lead, rides up on Black Bart's diversion in the desert: a single tollbooth in the middle of nowhere. Taggart looks at the sign and reads it aloud: "Lepetomane Thruway? Now what'll that asshole think of next?" He turns to his posse and asks, "Has anybody got a dime?" The men of the motley posse grumble and search their pockets. They come up empty. Taggart, exasperated, shouts, "Somebody's got to go back and get a shitload of dimes!"

The most raucous scene involving Taggart is arguably the infamous "farting" scene. Taggart enters the proceedings amid all the flatulence, and his sniffing of the air speaks for itself. Lyle looks up and says to him, "How about some more beans, Mr. Taggart?" Taggart fans his hat in the air and says to Lyle, "I'd say you had enough."

Korman is also at the top of his game here. He became part of Brooks's stock company with this film (he's equally hilarious as Dr. Seward in Brooks's *Dracula: Dead and Loving It*, 1995); and there's a good reason for that: his timing and sense of anarchy fit perfectly into Brooks's crazy world. His Hedley Lamarr is vain, vainglorious, and pompous; he's also impatient with the ineptitude that surrounds him.

When he instructs Taggart to obtain the services of "every vicious criminal and gunslinger in the west," he orders him to "[t]ake this down. I want rustlers, cutthroats, murderers, bounty hunters, desperados, mugs, pugs, thugs, nitwits, halfwits, dimwits, vipers, snipers, con men, Indian agents, Mexican bandits, muggers, buggerers, bushwackers, hornswogglers, horse thieves, bull dykes, train robbers, bank robbers, ass-kickers, shit-kickers, and Methodists."

Taggart is still reaching for his pen and paper by the end of this speech. "Could you repeat that, sir?" he asks timidly.

Also a good straight man when required, Korman manages to keep from cracking up—something he routinely failed to do on *The Carol Burnett Show* when Tim Conway was around, inevitably to the delight of the audience—during exchanges such as the one in which he is asking applicants for his gang about their qualifications. One particularly seedy-looking fellow (Bert Madrid) steps up from the line eagerly. Lamarr asks, "Qualifications?" The applicant replies, "Rape, murder, arson, and rape." Lamarr points out, "You said rape twice." The applicant smiles seedily and says, "I like rape." Again, a tasteless joke that probably wouldn't fly today.

Korman is also great at breaking the fourth wall, which is another trademark of Brooks's work. When he admonishes the assembled throng to go forth and cause chaos, he announces, "Men, you are about to embark on a great crusade to stamp out runaway decency in the west. Now, you men will only be risking your lives, whilst I will be risking an almost certain Academy Award nomination for Best Supporting Actor."

In an earlier scene, he completely obliterates the fourth wall when he says to himself, "A sheriff! But law and order is the last thing I want. Wait a minute—maybe I could turn this thing into my advantage. If I could find a sheriff who so offends the citizens of Rock Ridge that his very appearance would drive them out of town. . . . But where would I find such a man?" He turns to the camera: "Why am I asking you?"

Korman is just as good in the small, throwaway scenes, such as the one in which he sits in a bubble bath and suddenly starts acting like a three-year-old, asking Taggart where his "froggy" is. It's a remarkably silly scene that shouldn't work, but it does.

Taggart plunges his hand into the bubble bath, apparently grabbing something—but it isn't Lamarr's froggy. "Taggart!" Lamarr exclaims. Taggart looks contrite and says, "Sorry, sir."

And, of course, who could ever forget Lamarr's dying words during the anarchic climax as he looks at Douglas Fairbanks's picture in the forecourt of Grauman's Chinese Theater: "How did he do such fantastic stunts with such little feet?"

Korman also worked for Brooks in *High Anxiety* (1977), *History of the World, Part 1* (1981), the aforementioned *Dracula: Dead and Loving It*, and a short-lived TV series for Brooks called *The Nutt House* (1989), but he was never funnier than he was in *Blazing Saddles*. The lawsuit from Hedy Lamarr was well worth the trouble.

Another scene-stealer in *Blazing Saddles*—although he's a minor character who has little to do with the plot—is Mongo, as played by Karras. It was certainly the high point of his career, although he made over forty acting appearances in such movies as *Paper Lion* (1968), *Porky's* (1981), and *Against All Odds* (1984), as well as in episodes of such TV series as *The Odd Couple*, *Rowan and Martin's Laugh-In*, *M*A*S*H*, and many others. Mongo, however, is undoubtedly his best-remembered characterization, both for its silliness and its sweetness. The scene in which he rides into town on a bull is topped only by the later scene in which he punches the horse.

It's a credit to Karras's acting ability that he manages to make Mongo a more-than-one-dimensional character. When he says, "Mongo . . . only pawn in game of life," it's both hilarious and poignant. After Bart "outsmarts" him by fooling him with an exploding candygram (Bart notes, "Mongo was easy. The bitch was inventing the candygram; probably won't even give me credit for it."), Mongo goes over to the side of the good guys and ends up following Bart around like a puppy dog. In fact, he doesn't want to leave his side, as he announces, "Mongo no go. Mongo stay with Sheriff Bart. Sheriff Bart first man ever whip Mongo. Mongo impressed. Have deep feelings for Sheriff Bart."

Jim looks at Bart and says, "Uh-oh, Bart. I think Mongo here's taken a liking to you." Mongo blushes shyly and says, "Uh-uh, naw, Mongo straight!"

Mongo is cartoonish throughout, reminiscent of some of the old Looney Tunes characters; he would have made a great "dumb dog" in the old Warner Bros. cartoons, the kind who would say things like "I will rub him and squeeze him and call him George." In fact, the candygram scene is straight out of an old Looney Tunes or Merrie Melodies cartoon.

During one of Mongo's rampages, while the big guy is beating up a barroom full of wastrels and hooligans, Bart walks in dressed as a messenger boy and carrying a box. "Candygram for Mongo! Candygram for Mongo!" he announces. Mongo halts his carnage to turn to Bart and say, "Me Mongo." Bart tells him, "Sign, please," and hands him a pencil and a piece of paper on which Mongo makes some scratches and hands it back to Bart, who in turn hands the box to Mongo. Bart then turns, puts his fingers in his ears and walks out of the bar to the tune of the "Merrie Melodies" theme "Merrily We Roll Along." "Mongo like candy," says the big dumb brute and opens up the box, which goes *boom* in the best cartoon manner.

Of course, the biggest scene-stealer—who won an Oscar nomination for her troubles—is Madeline Kahn as Lili Von Shtüpp. Her impersonation of Dietrich is flawless; even her slightly off-key singing is spot-on. And so is her line delivery. Her chemistry with Little and Korman is especially choice.

As Brooks later wrote, "Madeline became part of a great stock company that I was unknowingly putting together for future films. Like writer/director Preston Sturges did in the 1940s, I was starting to gather brilliant performers who I could call on to do almost anything. There was Madeline, Gene Wilder, Harvey Korman, Dom DeLuise, and soon I would add the great Marty Feldman and Cloris Leachman."

Von Shtüpp's wildly over-the-top German accent at times borders on that of Elmer Fudd: she can't pronounce her "Rs." The uncut version of the film features the exchange between Von Shtüpp and Bart in the dark, and all we hear is Kahn's voice, plus one important sound effect. Von Shtüpp asks Bart seductively, "Tell me, schatze, is it twue what they say about the way you people are . . . gifted?" We then hear the sound of a zipper being opened, at which point Lili exclaims, "Oh, it's twue! It's twue! It's twue!"

Her stage performance is truly a showstopper. In between verses of "I'm Tired," she indulges in banter with members of the audience. One cowboy named Tex (Craig Littler) is enjoying her performance while in a very relaxed state, his feet propped up on the stage. Lili sees him and says, "Hello, cowboy, what's your name?" He replies, "Tex, ma'am."

"Texmam?" Lili asks him, "Well, Texmam, are you in show business?"
Tex replies, "Well, no."

She gives his feet a kick. "Then why don't you get your fwiggin' feet off the stage?"

Kahn is a constant delight throughout *Blazing Saddles*. She's funny, sexy, and delightfully over the top, commanding every scene she's in. One wishes that she was in the film more than she is, but Brooks's vision doesn't have much time for females, sadly. As the progenitor of so-called buddy movies, *Blazing Saddles* is a very male-centric movie.

The role of Jim, the Waco Kid, was a star-making one for Gene Wilder. To be sure, he had received critical acclaim for his performances in *Bonnie and Clyde*, *The Producers*, and *Start the Revolution without Me*, among other films, but none of those cemented him in the public mind like his role in *Blazing Saddles*. As Jim, his comic timing is impeccable—but that goes without saying. What makes his performance really remarkable is that despite all the lunacy and comedic anarchy, Wilder gives Jim an unexpected *pathos* that is only implied in the script. Wilder brings the character to full flower, and we root for this broken-down, alcoholic gunslinger from the very first moment we see him hanging upside down in the cell.

When Wilder cracks up Little with his ad-libbed "You know . . . morons" line, he cracks up the audience too. His delivery of every comedic line is brilliant, and he probably has more lines than Little. Sometimes Little acts as straight man to Wilder, as when Bart says, "I better go check out this Mongo character," and Jim tells him, "Oh, no, don't do that. If you shoot him, you'll just make him mad."

One can't imagine Gig Young in this role, and we should all thank the gods that Wilder was cast instead. Can you picture the exchange in which Bart asks him, "What's your name?" to which Jim replies, "Well, my name is Jim, but most people call me . . . Jim" with Young in the part? I thought not.

Jim, still hung over, is sitting in the sheriff's office with Bart when Bart asks him, "Well, Jim, since you're my guest and I'm your host, what's your pleasure. What do you like to do?"

Jim smiles wanly and replies, "Oh, I don't know. Play chess . . . screw."

Quickly, Bart responds, "Let's play chess!"

Then there's Jim's monologue about how he ended up in the lowly state in which Bart found him: "Well, it got so that every pissant prairie punk who thought he could shoot a gun would ride into town to try out the Waco Kid. I must have killed more men than Cecil B. DeMille. It got pretty gritty. I started to hear the word 'draw' in my sleep. Then one day, I was just walking down the street when I heard a voice behind me say, 'Reach for it, mister!' I spun around . . . and there I was, face to face with a six-year-old kid. Well, I just threw my guns down and walked away. Little bastard shot me in the ass. So I limped to the nearest saloon, crawled into a whiskey bottle . . . and I've been there ever since."

Again, a brilliant delivery, combining absurd, off-color humor with pathos.

Some of Jim's gags are visual. He says to Bart, "Look at my hand," then holds up his hand and keeps it level in front of him. "Steady as a rock," Bart says admiringly. "Yeah, but I shoot with this one," Jim informs him, holding up his other hand, which trembles as if he's in the midst of an earthquake.

The sadness of the character comes through in a very brief exchange after Jim guzzles down a bottle of whiskey all at once. Bart is properly horrified, and says to Jim, "A man drink like that and he don't eat, he is going to *die!*"

Jim looks at him and says, wanly yet eagerly, "When?"

We're with Jim all the way when he gets sober and decides maybe he's still the Waco Kid after all. One of the funniest and most poignant scenes occurs when Taggart, Lyle, and some of their cronies decide to "waste" Bart just because he's black. Jim stands nearby when Lyle commands, "All right, boys, on the count of three!"

Jim tells them calmly, "I wouldn't do that if I were you."

Lyle says to his men, "Don't pay no attention to that alkie. He can't even hold a gun, much less shoot it."

Jim blows on his fingertips as Lyle repeats, "Like I said, on the count of three. One . . . two . . . three!"

Jim draws with lightning speed, and the guns are shot out of the cowboys' hands in rapid succession. The next shot reveals Jim to be standing there calmly, his arms folded, smoke billowing out of his holsters.

Bart, who seems quite pleasantly surprised, says to the cowboys, "Well, don't just stand there lookin' stupid, graspin' your hands in pain." Bart draws his own gun as he says, "How about a little applause for the Waco Kid?"

Still in a state of semi-shock, the men burst into thunderous applause.

The sweetness—yes, there *is* sweetness in *Blazing Saddles*—reaches its zenith at the end of the picture, when Bart and Jim have finished watching the movie within the movie at Grauman's Chinese Theater. Bart suddenly ends up back in the western town, hopping on his palomino to slowly ride off into the sunset. He stops when he sees Jim, still munching on his popcorn from the theater.

Jim asks him, "Where you headed, cowboy?"

"Nowhere special," Bart replies.

Jim smiles wanly and muses, "Nowhere special . . . I've always wanted to go there."

Bart smiles and says, "Come on."

The two start to ride off on their horses, later exchanging them for a long black limousine, which drives them off into that big, beautiful western sunset.

As Brooks wrote in his autobiography, "Other directors may have broken the fourth wall, but I think in *Blazing Saddles*, I shattered it."

Wilder's portrayal of Jim, the Waco Kid, is one of the finest performances in any madcap comedy, bridging the gap between out-and-out farce and believability without any obvious patchwork. Wilder *is* the Waco Kid, but even more importantly, he's Jim, the alcoholic cowboy in search of redemption, and who ultimately finds it. If this sort of comedy had been more respected at the time, he probably would have received an Academy Award nomination. And perhaps in some alternate universe, where the fourth wall doesn't exist, he did.

As for Cleavon Little—portrayer of the titular character of the original screenplay—his biggest national exposure before *Blazing Saddles* had been in the series *Temperatures Rising*, and previous to that he had impressed viewers with a guest appearance on a 1971 episode of *All in the Family* in which he had played a burglar who broke into Archie Bunker's house. Little had an appealing, smooth charm and was a natural for comedy. His role as Bart saw him at the apex of his career, and, sadly, he never reached that pinnacle again. Yet Bart was enough to give him screen immortality and a select place in the pantheon of great comedic talent.

That easy-going charm made him perfect for the role of Bart, who must convince the people of Rock Ridge that he is qualified to maintain his position as sheriff. Little is pitch-perfect in the role, from his first appearance in front of the townspeople ("Excuse me while I whip this out," he tells them, causing them to gasp and then sigh with relief when he pulls out a piece of paper) to the hilarious scene in which Jim says to two members of the KKK, "Oh, boys! Lookee what I got here!" and pretends to capture Bart, who smiles at the Klansmen and says cheerily, "Hey, where the white women at?"

Little even excels at throwaway lines, such as when Charlie (Charles McGregor), upon hearing that Bart had been hanged and surprised at seeing him alive, says to him, "They said you was hung." Bart smiles at the double entendre and says, "And they was right!"

Earlier in the film, when Bart is trying to convince the townsfolk that he's qualified to be the sheriff, the Johnson clan load their guns and point them at him. Thinking quickly, Bart points his pistol at his own head. In a low voice, he proclaims he is going to shoot himself if anyone makes a move, as though he is his own hostage.

This absurd scene—loosely based on Brooks's own childhood experience with a water pistol—works only because the dim-wittedness of the Rock Ridge citizens has already been established. Olson Johnson (Huddleston) cautions, "Hold it, men. He's not bluffing." Dr. Sam Johnson (Richard Collier), shouts, "Listen to him, men! He's just crazy enough to do it!"

In his lower voice, Bart continues threatening to shoot his "hostage." Then, in a high-pitched, feminine voice, he exclaims, "Oh, lawdy, lawd, he's desperate! Do what he say, do what he say!"

At this point, the brain-dead townspeople drop their guns. Bart pushes the gun against his throat and drags himself through the crowd toward the sheriff's office. Harriet Johnson (Arthur), concerned, asks, "Isn't anybody going to help that poor man?" Her husband Sam shushes her, "Hush, Harriet! That's a sure way to get him killed!"

Again in his high-pitched voice, Bart screams, "Oooh, hep me, hep me, somebody hep me! Hep me! Hep me!" Then in his low voice, he growls (to himself), "Shut up!"

Bart places his hand over his own mouth and drags himself, struggling, into his office. Closing the door, he seems quite satisfied with his performance. "Oh, baby," he says to himself, "you are so talented." Then, looking into the camera, he says, "And they are so dumb!"

This scene, as insane as it is, is a perfect parody of every scene in every western—or crime thriller—in which a hostage has been taken by a bad guy. It's played with all the over-the-top relish it needs, and it's one of the funniest scenes in the film.

Through the first third of the film, Bart's plight seems fairly hopeless. When he cheerfully greets an elderly woman (Jessamine Milner) on the street with, "Mornin,' Ma'am. And isn't it a lovely mornin'?," her terse retort is "Up yours, n----r." This always got a huge laugh in 1974. But would it get such a reaction in the twenty-first century?

And here we have a classic example of the problems *Blazing Saddles* would have today, should anyone want to—Heaven help us—remake it. Times change and what is acceptable and unacceptable change. In the early seventies, when popular TV shows explored racism like never before, complete with usages of just about every other racial or ethnic epithet there was, very little was forbidden, especially in motion pictures. If you could hear those words on network television, what you could hear and see in a movie theater was, well, almost anything you could think of. It's difficult to imagine audiences in the twenty-first century watching hard-core porn films in a public theater, but that was common in the seventies. So were all the four-letter words that had ever been uttered, along with racial and ethnic insults.

Here is the point, however: in the case of *Blazing Saddles*, and indeed of blaxploitation movies and other "urban" fare in the 1970s, racial epithets were hurled ironically. In other words, racism itself was being parodied. Just as Archie Bunker was shown to be, in creator Norman Lear's words, "a real horse's ass," so were racists in most films. John Shaft, played by Richard Roundtree, was smarter than most white cops. *Foxy Brown* (1974) starred the statuesque Pam Grier as a black female avenger. Movies such as *In the Heat of the Night* had paved the way for such an anti-racist backlash and black audiences were being pandered to in mainstream movies *en masse* for the first time. Although low-budget films had been made exclusively for black audiences in the 1930s and 1940s, they were aimed strictly at minority audiences, and the content was inoffensive. As many as five hundred so-called race films were produced between 1915 and 1952, and most of them were produced by white-owned companies outside of Hollywood. Some black-owned studios existed then, such as Lincoln Motion Picture Company, originally based in Omaha, Nebraska, and the Chicago-based Micheaux Film Company, but they were few and far between. In the American South, these films played at racially segregated theaters. It was rare for films such as *Harlem on the Prairie* (1937) or *Dirty Gertie from Harlem USA* (1946) to be shown to white audiences, and many were shown by white-owned theaters in the North only at midnight shows or matinees.

Race films were produced mainly in northern cities, where their target audiences consisted of poor southern blacks who had moved northward. Despite their all-black casts, common storylines involved the so-called improvement of the black race, the disputes between educated and uneducated African Americans, and the tragic outcome for those who resisted white middle-class values.

Harlem on the Prairie is especially interesting, and in many ways it's a direct ancestor of *Blazing Saddles*. Its star, Herbert Jeffrey, was at the time a popular singer with the Earl "Fatha" Hines Band, a jazz band that comprised up to twenty-eight members onstage. Known for his baritone voice, Jeffrey (a.k.a. "Herb Jeffries" when he was singing) originally came up with the idea of an all-black cowboy movie and initially intended to have the film distributed to movie houses in the South that catered to black audiences. White cowboy star Gene Autry stepped in to help him, however, and together they succeeded in making a deal with a Dallas-based company called Sack Amusements to distribute the film nationally. The film premiered in Los Angeles at the Paramount Theater and in New York at the Rialto in December of 1937.

With Jeffrey starring as the cowboy hero Jeff Kincaid—to whom Black Bart certainly owed a debt of gratitude—*Harlem on the Prairie* was filmed on location at the Iverson Ranch in Chatsworth, California, and the Walker Ranch in Newhall, California, for less than $50,000—a very low budget indeed. The film served to correct the then-popular image of an all-white Old West and revealed to audiences that there were, indeed, black cowboys.

The plot was typical of an old-time western: Kincaid is employed by a pretty young woman (Consuelo Harris) to locate lost gold. Along the way, there's plenty of romance, comedy, melodrama, and song, the latter of which is provided by Jeffrey, including the title song and a then-popular tune called "Romance in the Rain." Most of the comedy was provided by the ubiquitous Mantan Moreland, who was known for his valuable comic relief in countless mainstream movies such as *King of the Zombies* (1941), *The Strange Case of Dr. Rx*, and *Tarzan's New York Adventure* (both 1942), among many other movies of the era. Moreland, a gifted comic actor, worked up until the end of his life in 1973, with his last film being *The Young Nurses*, released in that year.

Helmed by legendary B movie director Sam Newfield (*Lost Continent*, 1951, among many others), *Harlem on the Prairie* was so successful that it spawned three sequels, *Two-Gun Man from Harlem* (1938), *Harlem Rides the Range*, and *The Bronze Buckaroo* (both 1939). The latter three renamed the lead character Bob Blake, however, due to a copyright issue. Under any name, Jeffrey (or Jeffries) was the star, and his singing and acting career flourished during the forties and fifties; he passed away in 2014 at the ripe old age of one hundred.

His successor, Cleavon Little, was sadly not so fortunate. In a sense, Black Bart was the direct descendant of Jeff Kincaid. Little's career, however, was not as charmed as Jeffrey's nor was his life anywhere near as long. The Hollywood establishment never knew quite what to do with Little and, to a certain extent, his remarkable talent was wasted. *Blazing Saddles* turned out to be his one shot at real stardom, but, for whatever reason, he never became the household name he should have been. Ironically, Richard Pryor became a huge star in part because of the films he did with Wilder, but his replacement in *Blazing Saddles* was usually relegated to secondary roles in less than stellar vehicles such as *FM* (1978), *Scavenger Hunt* (1979), and *Once Bitten* (1985). Most of his later work was divided between stage and television, and he appeared in such TV series as *True Colors*, *Bagdad Café*, and *MacGyver*. He died in 1992 from colon cancer at the tragically young age of fifty-three. In a case of further irony, his final television appearance was in an episode of *Tales from the Crypt* titled "This'll Kill Ya."

Nevertheless, Little's legacy in the history of comedy films is a potent one. *Blazing Saddles* is now considered to be one of the greatest comedy films of all time and one of the funniest movies ever made. It's often been compared to *Duck Soup* (1933), the most anarchic of the Marx Brothers movies, and that's no small potatoes. In a 2017 interview by Rebecca Jones for the BBC, Brooks postulated that *Blazing Saddles* could never be made today. "It's okay not to hurt the feelings of various tribes and groups," he said. "However, it's not good for comedy." Brooks continued, "Comedy has to walk a thin line, take risks. It's the lecherous little elf whispering in the king's ear, telling the truth about human behavior."

In the interview, Brooks wanted to make one thing perfectly clear: "I personally would never touch gas chambers or the death of children or Jews at the hands of the Nazis. In no way is that useable or correct for comedy. It's just in truly bad taste." Brooks went on to say that that was the "only thing" he would avoid and that "[e]verything else is okay." Brooks also mentioned in the interview that he was interested in turning *Blazing Saddles* into a Broadway musical, as "[i]t's practically a musical anyway, it has so many numbers in it."

While Brooks's idea of turning *Blazing Saddles* into a stage musical is currently in limbo, he's quite right in that the film could probably not be remade today. At least, not in the way it was made in the seventies. One reason is indeed political correctness, as Brooks lamented to Bill Maher on HBO's *Real Time with Bill Maher*:

Isn't it strange? It could hardly be made then. Certainly not ten years before then. And now it's suddenly 40 years later, it cannot be made today. That's weird. The prejudices or whatever, the restrictions, should have thoroughly diluted by now, and here we are—it's amazing. We're playing it safe. I don't think the individual person is playing it safe, but I think the organizations—let's call them television networks or studios—they're playing it safe. They don't want to get sued. They don't want to lose the Latino endorsement or the black endorsement or the Jewish endorsement.

Brooks is correct, of course—but only up to a point. In a piece highlighting Brooks's interview with Maher, Andrew Roberts, entertainment writer for the website UPROXX.com, wrote in 2015,

Pick up any text about the period (1974) and you're hit with talk of the "New Hollywood" and the collapse of the bloated studio system that bled money during the "golden years" of Hollywood. It was a time to take those risks you hear guys like Coppola and Stallone talk about. There was a search for that brand new method of success and features like *Blazing Saddles* could thrive there.

Fast forward to today and it's a different situation. Blockbusters carved out their stake, conglomerates snatched up media properties left and right, leaving independent film to fill the role of the New Hollywood. Now studios produce films that will net them the most profit on a global scale, boosting the stock of a parent company that may resemble a fanged, tentacled beast.

Roberts concludes his piece with a positive outlook: "The good thing is, we don't need another *Blazing Saddles*. We have one and it's great. That should be the biggest reason we don't need one today; it doesn't have to happen. A musical, maybe, but the films [from that era] are fine the way they are."

Roberts is right on the money, which is to say, it's all about money. We have enough inferior remakes around already. There have been recent versions of such seventies classics as *Straw Dogs*, *The Heartbreak Kid*, *Get Carter*, and *The Goodbye Girl*, most of which have failed both critically and commercially. What would be the point of remaking *Blazing Saddles?* It sets such a high bar that any remake would be along the lines of remaking *Duck Soup*, *Horse Feathers*, or, for that matter, *Citizen Kane*. It would be utterly pointless, and the only hope of such a project would be to make money by trading off the name of the original.

Now that we've settled that argument, let's take a look at the one and only *Blazing Saddles* through the lens of its most important creative force, Brooks himself, and what he did with the concept in 1974. There had never been a film quite like it before, even in Brooks's own oeuvre. His first two features, *The Producers* and *The Twelve Chairs*, had been loud, bombastic, and bold, but nothing in them indicated the wild, utter lunacy that was *Blazing Saddles*. The closest either of them came to that sort of out-of-control zaniness was the "Springtime for Hitler" show-within-a-film in *The Producers*. But sustaining that sort of madness and anarchy throughout an entire feature didn't seem possible—until February 1974, when *Blazing Saddles* exploded into an unsuspecting world.

As a film buff, Brooks stole from the best. *Blazing Saddles* parodies the great and not-so-great Hollywood westerns to a T, with homages to everything from *Destry Rides Again* to *High Noon*. Interestingly enough, it borrows a number of plot points—and perhaps part of its title—from an obscure B-movie western called *Saddles and Sagebrush* that had been made by Columbia Pictures thirty years earlier. The 1943 oater—directed by William Berke and starring Russell Hayden, Dub Taylor, and Ann Savage—had featured numerous songs (provided by a group called Bob Wills and His Texas Playboys); and its plot had involved an unscrupulous land-grabber (William Wright) who, with his gang of henchmen, incurs the ire of local ranch owners. Needless to say, the hero, Lucky Randall (Hayden) takes care of the situation (aided by the singing cowboys) and good emerges triumphant.

Elements of *Saddles and Sagebrush* may have been in the back of Brooks's mind—the chances are very good that he had seen the film in his younger days—but even stronger elements of a much more recent western may have been at the forefront, although as far as I know, Brooks has never acknowledged this: key plot points seem to have been taken from Clint Eastwood's *High Plains Drifter*, which had been released in April of 1973.

High Plains Drifter was written by Ernest Tidyman (*The French Connection*, 1971) and was an allegorical western with strong supernatural overtones. The film, directed by and starring Eastwood, concerned a mysterious stranger who seems to be an avenging angel, taking vengeance on a small town that was complicit in the murder of its previous sheriff. The town of Lago has some similarities to Rock Ridge, except that its occupants, rather than being criminally stupid, are instead accomplices to murder.

As with *Blazing Saddles*, there's a prominent preacher (Robert Donner), who, instead of spouting silly lines, pronounces "God" as "Gawd" and generally comes across as vapid and hypocritical. Of course, it's hard to imagine Donner's character behaving in quite the same way as Liam Dunn's Reverend Johnson and spouting such lines as "Now I don't have to tell you good folks what's been happening in our little town. Sheriff murdered, crops burned, stores looted, people stampeded, and cattle raped. The time has come to act, and act fast. I'm leaving."

All of those things happen in *High Plains Drifter* as well—except maybe for the cattle being raped. It does seem at times that Brooks was having a little fun with the darker elements of Eastwood's film, especially with the plot point in which the stranger gets all the townspeople to paint what's left of the town blood-red and then lures the three main villains there to kill off most of the townspeople; in Brooks's film, Bart gets all the townspeople of Rock Ridge to build an exact copy of the town, which is then attacked by the villains. The good (but stupid) people of Rock Ridge help to defeat the bad guys, so the darkness of *High Plains Drifter*—a controversial western at the time—is turned on its head.

As for movies that directly influenced the style of *Blazing Saddles*, I don't think there can be any doubt that Brooks saw Bud Yorkin's *Start the Revolution without Me*, in which Wilder costarred with Donald Sutherland. A farce loosely derived from such classic tales as Charles Dickens's *A Tale of Two Cities* and Alexandre Dumas's *The Corsican Brothers*, Yorkin's film, released early in 1970, foreshadowed *Blazing Saddles* in many ways; in some respects, it's the *Blazing Saddles* of costume epics.

Lavishly filmed in France, *Start the Revolution without Me* follows the adventures of two sets of identical twins separated at birth. The bulk of the story takes place in 1789—which the narrator (Walker Edmiston) hilariously reminds us of at least twenty times—at the time of the French Revolution, and the two sets of twins find themselves involved in palace intrigue, among other situations stolen from just about every period piece you've ever encountered, including *The Man in the Iron Mask*.

The movie features a wonderful cast of British and European actors, including Hugh Griffith, Billie Whitelaw, Jack MacGowran, Victor Spinetti, Ewa Aulin, Murray Melvin, and Graham Stark. Orson Welles even gets into the act, as the on-screen host of the enterprise.

In many ways, *Start the Revolution without Me* feels like a warm-up for *Blazing Saddles* in its broadly farcical, sometimes downright silly approach. Yorkin, who made this film with his production partner Norman Lear, would later be associated with such Lear-produced television programs as *All in the Family* and *Sanford and Son*, and in this film, he shows a real flair for the absurd.

At times, Wilder lives up to his surname by going wildly over the top in *Start the Revolution without Me*, as he did in *The Producers* and would later do in Brooks's *Young Frankenstein*, but in a good way. Nobody goes crazy quite like Wilder, and you always have the feeling he's just been unleashed from the rubber room and is now free to do any outrageous thing he wants. The surprise is Sutherland, whose more subtle comic touches are just as endearing. Sight gags run fast and furiously, and as film critic Gene Siskel wrote, the movie is "a terribly funny parody of the over-stuffed eighteenth century costume dramas that crowd the vaults of many a major studio."

It's also sumptuously produced, as Charles Champlin wrote in the *Los Angeles Times*: "An absolutely gorgeous piece of costume cookery, a dazzling and sustained farce which is also a mad, affectionate tribute to every *epee* epic, every sabre-and-sex, bodice-and-bodkin historical melodrama anybody ever saw."

While *Start the Revolution without Me* was not a huge box-office hit, its positive notices must have impressed Brooks—who undoubtedly viewed it upon release, as it starred Wilder—and he probably thought, "If Yorkin can get away with this stuff, why not me?"

The genius of Brooks is in the confidence of his third feature film: from the opening frames, which make the movie look, feel, and sound like a fifties Technicolor western, to the final shot of our heroes riding off into the sunset, there's nary a wrong step. Brooks's anarchy is evident in every shot, every line of dialogue, every music cue.

The myriad references for the film buffs are funny whether or not you know the movies that are being parodied. When a Mexican bandit laughs and says, "Badges? We don't need no stinkin' badges," it is of course a reference to the same line in John Huston's *The Treasure of the Sierra Madre* (1948), but it's funny whether or not you know where the line comes from.

Then there are the just plain silly moments, such as the exchange between Bart (who is disguised as a Klansman) explaining his qualifications as a bad guy to Lamarr: "Stampeding cattle," he announces. "That's not much of a crime," says Lamarr. "Through the Vatican?" counters Bart. Lamarr smiles wanly and says, "Kinky . . . "

Lamarr then tells Bart, "Sign here," offering him a pen and paper. Bart reaches out, exposing his black hands. Jim, who is standing nearby, admonishes him: "Why, Rhett! How many times have I told you to wash up after the weekly cross burning?" Jim licks his own fingers, then rubs Bart's hand as if to clean it. "See, it's coming off," Jim says. Taggart, standing next to Bart, whips off the Klan hood, exposing Bart for all to see. Nonplussed, Bart exclaims, "Now for my next impression . . . Jesse Owens!" He runs off at Olympic speed.

The height of silliness is achieved during the "swearing in" ceremony, when Lamarr tells the assembled cutthroats, "Repeat after me. I . . ." and the men repeat, "I . . . " The rest of it goes like this:

> **Lamarr:** . . . Your name . . .
>
> **Men:** . . . Your name . . .
>
> **Lamarr:** (under his breath) Schmucks. (to the men) Pledge allegiance . . .
>
> **Men:** Pledge allegiance . . .
>
> **Lamarr:** . . . to Hedley Lamarr . . .
>
> **Men:** . . . to Hedy Lamarr . . .
>
> **Lamarr:** That's Hedley!
>
> **Men:** That's Hedley!
>
> **Lamarr:** And to the evil . . .
>
> **Men:** And to the evil . . .
>
> **Lamarr:** . . . for which he stands.
>
> **Men:** . . . for which he stands.
>
> **Lamarr:** Now go do that voodoo that you do so well!

Some of the silliest non sequiturs are reserved for Brooks himself as Governor Lepetomane. After he gets nearly everyone in the room to say "Harrumph," he points to the one member of his cabinet who failed to do so. "I didn't get a harrumph out of that guy!" he complains.

Lamarr: "Give the governor harrumph!" The politician (George Dockstader) gives him the required "Harrumph." Lepetomane admonishes him: "You watch your ass." Ever the sycophant, Lamarr says to everyone, "Gentlemen, please rest your sphincters," to which Lepetomane concurs, "Well put."

Then, of course, there's the politically incorrect byplay with his secretary (Hilton), whose revealing outfit prevents Lepetomane from concentrating on his work, whatever that is. The governor is having trouble placing his pen back in its holder and asks Lamarr to help put his pen back. Lamarr tells him to just think of his secretary and Lepetomane puts the pen right in with no problem—naughty.

The greatest madness of all, though, is reserved for the final sequence, in which the fighting cowboys literally break the fourth wall and find themselves on the next studio set, which happens to be a Busby Berkeley–type musical in which the very fey dancers are performing the song "The French Mistake." Their leader, Buddy Bizarre (DeLuise) is horrified by their appearance, and shouts, "What are you doing here? This is a closed set!"

"Piss on you!" Taggart shouts back. "I'm working for Mel Brooks!"

Taggart prepares to punch Buddy. "Not in the face!" Buddy screams.

Taggart obliges by punching him in the stomach. Out of breath and collapsing, Buddy manages to say, "Thank you."

It's difficult to overstate just how insane *Blazing Saddles* was to audiences in early 1974. The surrealistic satirical humor of *Monty Python's Flying Circus* didn't appear on American TV screens (courtesy of Public Broadcasting Service [PBS]) until later that year, and, aside from Woody Allen movies such as *Sleeper* (1972) and a few others of that ilk, American audiences at the time were far more used to the comedy of

Lucille Ball and Bob Hope than they were to this kind of wild, zany, and downright silly comedy. Way back in 1933, the Marx Brothers movie *Duck Soup*—now widely regarded as the team's masterpiece—had proven to be too far out for most American audiences (it didn't play well in Peoria, as the saying goes); and the movie lost money—and lost the Marx Brothers their contract with Paramount. Their later films had less of *Duck Soup*'s anarchic humor and more music to compensate.

In that respect, Brooks was taking a big chance with *Blazing Saddles*. Would it play in Peoria? The answer to that was a resounding *yes*. Times had changed, the culture had changed and the wildness of the sixties had paved the way for Brooks's style of unbridled nonsense. The age of irony, and of movie parodies, had arrived.

Again, the American Film Institute (AFI) lists *Blazing Saddles* as the sixth funniest film on their "100 Years . . . 100 Laughs" list. Let's take a closer look at that list.

The criteria for a film's inclusion on the list are as follows: the movie must be feature length (over sixty minutes); it must be an American film; it must be funny (duh!); and it must have what the AFI calls "laughs that echo across time, enriching America's film heritage and inspiring artists and audiences today." Now let's take a quick look at the five movies that this august body considers to be funnier than *Blazing Saddles*.

Number one on the list is Billy Wilder's 1959 black-and-white classic *Some Like It Hot*. Written by Wilder's frequent collaborator I. A. L. Diamond, this "crime comedy" stars Marilyn Monroe, Jack Lemmon, and Tony Curtis and concerns two musicians who disguise themselves as women to escape from the clutches of gangsters who they have witnessed committing a crime. *Some Like It Hot* is highly regarded both by critics and audiences and received six Academy Award nominations, winning one for Best Costume Design. But is it funny?

It's very funny indeed, and it broke a number of taboos of the time as it was produced outside the auspices of the Production Code, with its themes of cross-dressing and implied homosexuality considered to be too "hot" for the code. It's a sophisticated bedroom farce, and the film's closing line uttered by Joe E. Brown when he discovers that the "woman" he loves is actually a man—and he looks at the camera saying, "Nobody's perfect!"—is ranked #78 on *The Hollywood Reporter* list of 100 favorite movie lines.

Some Like It Hot is directed with consummate skill, written with dry wit, and performed to near perfection. But is it as funny as *Blazing Saddles*? As brilliant as it is, *Some Like It Hot* is a bit more cerebral in its humor and, as such, doesn't achieve the belly laughs of Brooks's equally brilliant parody. To this writer, *Blazing Saddles* is the funnier film.

Number two on AFI's list is Sydney Pollack's *Tootsie* (1982). Apparently, the AFI finds cross-dressing to be hilarious, as *Tootsie* tells the high-spirited tale of a talented but "difficult" actor (Dustin Hoffman) whose inability to land jobs leads him to identify as a woman. Another critically acclaimed film, *Tootsie* won a Best Supporting Actress Oscar for Jessica Lange.

Pollack didn't have quite the flair for comedy that Wilder did; he seemed more at ease with weighty topics such as *They Shoot Horses, Don't They* (1969) and *Out of Africa* (1985, for which he won Best Director and Best Picture). As a result, *Tootsie* tempers its humor with social commentary; it pokes fun at everything from soap operas to sexism, from business agents to Manhattan snobbery. But is it funny?

BLAZING SADDLES MEETS YOUNG FRANKENSTEIN

It's funny in a very different way from *Blazing Saddles*. Hoffman is terrific in the lead, and the screenplay by Larry Gelbart and Murray Schisgal sparkles with witty dialogue. If you're expecting the kind of guffaws that most people get from Brooks's madcap vision, though, you may be disappointed. *Tootsie* is more the kind of movie that makes a wry smile appear on your lips rather than eliciting a hearty laugh-out-loud response. It has the warmth that *Blazing Saddles* never even tries for, but is it as funny? Not to this writer.

Number three on the AFI list is Stanley Kubrick's *Dr. Strangelove* (1964), a brilliant Cold War satire; some would say it is *the* definitive Cold War satire, with its subtitle *How I Learned to Stop Worrying and Love the Bomb*, an indication of the darkness of its humor. Written by Kubrick, Terry Southern, and Peter George, based on the book *Red Alert* by George, *Dr. Strangelove* stars Peter Sellers in three roles, along with a supporting cast that includes George C. Scott, Sterling Hayden, Tracy Reed, Keenan Wynn, James Earl Jones, and none other than Slim Pickens ten years before he played Taggart in *Blazing Saddles*.

In 1998, the AFI named *Dr. Strangelove* #26 in their list of the greatest American films of all time. But is it funny?

With its ridicule of planning for nuclear war, its savage skewering of the U.S. military, and its groundbreaking satire of myriad sacred cows, *Dr. Strangelove* is an important and powerful movie. Uber-critic Roger Ebert called it "the greatest political satire of the century." Indeed, the scene in which Major T. J. "King" Kong (Pickens) rides the H-bomb to its destination while hooting and hollering cowboy-style has become iconic.

Pickens is perhaps the funniest character in the film, which should come as no surprise if one has seen *Blazing Saddles* first. But there's no opportunity for him to be as hilarious in *Dr. Strangelove* as he is in Brooks's movie.

This is because *Dr. Strangelove* is, after all, a *black* comedy, but not because it has a black hero; it's because it finds humor in the possibility that the entire planet may be destroyed by monomaniacal human beings. The film's ending shows Dr. Strangelove (Sellers) exclaiming, "I can walk" after being in a wheelchair throughout the film and then combines shots of actual nuclear explosions, with English singer Vera Lynn crooning "We'll Meet Again" on the soundtrack. It's all very cerebral, very witty, and very, very dark. The original ending of *Dr. Strangelove*, vetoed by Kubrick, involved a *Blazing Saddle*–styled pie fight between the principal characters. It would have been quite something to have seen distinguished actors like Scott and Hayden involved in slapstick comedy, but Kubrick decided against it because of the scene's farcical nature, which he claimed would work against the pointed satire of the rest of the film.

I've never met anyone who laughed out loud at *Dr. Strangelove*—not one person. As for *Blazing Saddles*, on the two occasions I saw it in a cinema, much of the dialogue was drowned out by raucous laughter. So, as far as I'm concerned, *Blazing Saddles* is funnier than *Dr. Strangelove*—maybe not as carefully crafted, or as intelligent, but funnier.

Woody Allen's *Annie Hall* (1977) is number four on the list. Allen's satirical yet romantic comedy is certainly one of his best, and that's saying a lot. It was a major turning point in his career as a director, in which he graduated from the farcical nature of his earlier films such as *Bananas* (1971) and *Sleeper* (1973) to a more realistic look at Allen's Jewish identity, its subtext regarding psychoanalysis, and its deeper look at love and sexuality. *Annie Hall* was nominated for five Oscars and won four: Best Picture, Best Director, Best Actress in a Leading Role (Diane Keaton), and Best Original Screenplay (Allen and Marshall Brickman).

Critically acclaimed and a huge box-office success, *Annie Hall* is undoubtedly a great movie and a charming, intelligent, and warm comedy. But is it funny?

Well, sure it is. It's interesting, though, to note what critics of the time said of the movie, comparing it to Ingmar Bergman's *Scenes from a Marriage* (1973) and noting that it was "Allen's most closely focused and daring film to date." Those critiques don't exactly proclaim the movie to be a yock-fest. It's a very different kind of comedy from *Blazing Saddles*, that's for sure: adult, sophisticated, and oh so intelligent.

Allen's role as Alvy Singer, a stereotypically neurotic Jewish male, is contrasted with Keaton's Oscar-winning turn as his WASP-y, rather eccentric opposite. The film is as much a love letter to New York City as it is to Keaton, who was Allen's significant other at the time. There's no question that *Annie Hall* looms large as a classic romantic comedy, but it doesn't have the kind of belly laughs that *Blazing Saddles* has in almost every frame. It's funny, it's witty, and even wise, but, viewed today, it's more dated than Brooks's movie, as relationships between men and women have evolved over the years—and the clothing and hair styles certainly date it at 1977. In summary, *Annie Hall* is a fine film and a gem of a comedy, but is it as funny as *Blazing Saddles?* Not even close.

The AFI's number five funniest movie of all time is the Marx Brothers' *Duck Soup* (1933). Now you're talking. Ostensibly written by Bert Kalmar and Harry Ruby (with additional dialogue credited to Arthur Sheekman and Nat Perrin), *Duck Soup* is a comedy masterpiece. In the wild, anarchic plot, the newly installed president Rufus T. Firefly (Groucho) of the mythical nation of Fredonia has problems with the neighboring country of Sylvania, exacerbated by Sylvanian spies (Chico and Harpo) who are aiding their ambassador (Louis Calhern). As relations with the two countries deteriorate, the final moments of the film find them going to war with each other.

Although *Duck Soup* was somewhat ahead of its time in many ways, it's now widely considered to be the greatest film featuring the Marx Brothers. Its political satire is still right on the money, as witnessed by the comparisons of nationalism to a minstrel show, featuring a variation on the old Negro spiritual "All God's Chillun Got Wings," whose lyrics were altered to "All God's chillun got guns."

I can't imagine anything more timely for the United States in the twenty-first century. *Duck Soup* is more than political satire, however: its sight gags are second to none. There's the famous "mirror scene" involving Chico and Groucho, the uproarious scenes between Harpo and the street vendor (Edgar Kennedy), and a sequence that makes a jab at the Hays Code in which Harpo is seen in bed with a horse, while a woman sleeps in the bed next to them.

It would be impossible to describe the preposterous buffoonery, cynicism, and brilliance of *Duck Soup* by simply writing about it; you have to see the movie. Contrary to what has been claimed by some, it was not a box-office failure, although it didn't perform as well as the previous Marx Brothers film, *Horse Feathers* (1932). As directed by Leo McCarey, however—and the directors of the Marx Brothers pretty much let their stars do what they wanted—*Duck Soup* is relentless in its sheer lunacy, so much so that audiences during the Great Depression didn't really know what to make of it. As film historian Leonard Maltin wrote in his book *The Great Movie Comedians*, "Many right-thinkers laughed themselves silly in 1933—but a large number didn't. . . . The unrelieved assault of Marxian comedy was too much for some people." Film critic Daniel Griffin has compared *Duck Soup* to Charlie Chaplin's *The Great Dictator* (1940) and even to *Dr. Strangelove*, adding that it's "more unnerving in that *Duck Soup* doesn't seem to realize it is anything more than innocent fluff."

Duck Soup is funny. It's laugh-out-loud, belly laugh funny. Whether it's Groucho verbally sparring with, well, anyone, or just plain insulting Margaret Dumont ("Married . . . I can see you right now, in the kitchen, bending over a hot stove. But I can't see the stove.") or any of the intentionally silly songs (The "Fredonia National Anthem," which takes off on "The Star-Spangled Banner"), *Duck Soup* is utterly brilliant and utterly side-splitting. It is, in fact—as far as I'm concerned, anyway—the only other comedy that can match *Blazing Saddles* in sheer nonstop laughs.

According to Brooks, one day during the production of *Blazing Saddles*, as the cast and crew were breaking for lunch, Brooks happened to notice Wilder leaning against the wall of the sheriff's office set. He was scribbling something on a note pad. When Brooks asked Wilder to join him for lunch, he told him without looking up from his note pad, "In a minute, I have to finish a thought I have." When Brooks asked him what he was writing, he held out the notepad to him.

At the top of the pad, he had written "Young Frankenstein." When Brooks asked him what that was, Wilder told him that it was an idea for a movie about Baron Frankenstein's grandson, who, although seemingly an uptight scientist, is just as crazy as any member of the Frankenstein family. To create life is in his blood, but he doesn't know it yet.

Brooks was intrigued. He asked Wilder what his dream was for this potential movie. He told him that his dream was for Brooks to write it with him and direct it. And that is part two of our story of the remarkable year of Mel Brooks.

Part II

YOUNG FRANKENSTEIN

7

"HOW I DID IT"

The way Wilder told it in his autobiography *Kiss Me Like a Stranger*, he came up with the idea for *Young Frankenstein* while on vacation in Westhampton Beach. "After lunch one afternoon," he wrote, "I walked up to my bedroom with a yellow legal pad and a blue felt pen. At the top of the page, I wrote *Young Frankenstein* and then wrote two pages of what might happen if I were the great-grandson of Beaufort von Frankenstein and was called to Transylvania because I had just inherited the Frankenstein estate.

"Why the word 'Young' before the name 'Frankenstein'? It came out almost unconsciously, but when I asked myself later where that thought came from, I remembered Mickey Rooney in the film *Young Edison*, which I saw when I was a boy. Then I remembered a more recent clue: Anne Bancroft had made a film called *Young Winston*."

Young Winston had been critically acclaimed upon its release in 1972. It starred Simon Ward, known mainly at the time for his role in Terence Fisher's *Frankenstein Must Be Destroyed* (1969) opposite Peter Cushing as Baron Frankenstein—an irony indeed—as the young Winston Churchill. Directed by Richard Attenborough, *Young Winston* also starred Bancroft as Churchill's mother, Robert Shaw as Lord Randolph Churchill, John Mills as Lord Kitchener, and Anthony Hopkins as David Lloyd George. It was one of the most popular films at the British box office in 1972 and Ward was nominated for the Most Promising Male Newcomer Award at that year's Golden Globes (he lost to Edward Albert for *Butterflies Are Free*).

Wilder's idea, then, would be both a spoof of classic Frankenstein films and would additionally have the "snob appeal" of name-checking a recent critical and popular hit. It seemed like a win-win.

According to Brooks, after Wilder told him that his dream was that Brooks would collaborate on the script of what he called *Young Frankenstein* and agree to direct it, Brooks's first question was "You got any money on you?" Wilder told him he had $57. Brooks told him he'd take it as a down payment on writing *Young Frankenstein* with him, and that if he liked it, he would direct it.

As Brooks wrote in his memoirs, "That night, I went over to Gene's bungalow, at the Hotel Bel-Air, to discuss the concept. We stayed up until the early hours of the morning talking about the storyline over Earl Grey tea and English digestive biscuits. We talked about being very faithful to the tempo and the look of James Whale's marvelous black-and-white films, *Frankenstein* from 1931 and *The Bride of Frankenstein* from 1935."

When Whale's *Frankenstein* had been released by Universal in 1931, a few months after Tod Browning's *Dracula*, which had made a star of Bela Lugosi, it created a sensation and consolidated the horror film as a genre unto itself. Originally, Lugosi was to have played the monster in *Frankenstein*, but after several failed makeup tests, the Hungarian-born actor opted out; he also complained that the role lacked dialogue, and, after he had taken the time to learn English—although his thick Hungarian accent was part of his charm—he felt that to play a role without dialogue was something of an insult. "I was a star in my country," he complained, "and I will not be a scarecrow over here."

The role of the monster went instead to Whale's fellow Brit, Boris Karloff, born William Henry Pratt, who, like Lugosi, was in his forties and already a busy character actor with many film roles behind him, including that of a sinister mesmerist in a 1926 silent film called *The Bells*. The actor's unique, almost cadaverous bone structure fascinated Whale, and his facial features were built upon by Universal's premier makeup artist Jack Pierce to create the iconic visage of the monster that we all know today.

Colin Clive, who had starred the previous year in Whale's *Journey's End*—a highly successful drama at the time—was cast as Henry Frankenstein. In Mary Shelley's 1818 novel upon which the film was based, Frankenstein's first name was Victor, but, for whatever reason, it was changed to Henry—the first name of his best friend in the novel—while Victor became the name of his best friend in the film as played by a sincere but rather wooden Jon Boles. Frankenstein's fiancée Elizabeth was portrayed by Mae Clarke, whose main claim to fame at the time was having had a grapefruit pushed into her face by Jimmy Cagney in William A. Wellman's gangster drama *The Public Enemy*, released earlier in 1931.

Despite the Hays Code not being enforced in 1931, various state censor boards across the country trimmed certain scenes, specifically the infamous sequence in which the monster tosses a little girl (Marilyn Harris) into a lake, where she drowns. The resultant cut gave an inference of, perhaps, child molestation that Whale never intended.

Another cut was imposed by some states at the penultimate moment of the "creation" scene, in which an ecstatic Henry Frankenstein cries out, "It's alive! It's alive! Oh, in the name of God, now I know what it feels like to *be* God!" That last line was cut on the grounds of "blasphemy."

Whale's film essentially captured the spirit of Shelley's novel, while updating the period to the present day to take advantage of the spectacular electrical machinery constructed especially for the film by Kenneth Strickfaden. The setting in a strange European hinterland (the novel was set in Switzerland) became the famous and beloved backdrop for nearly all of Universal's gothic horror films.

The British-born Whale, who had shown up in Hollywood only a few years previously, gave an English sensibility to *Frankenstein* and, at the same time, a more Germanic look than Browning had brought to *Dracula*. Key elements taken from the novel were filmed with great care, such as the monster's assault on Elizabeth, but the story itself was condensed, deriving mostly from the various stage versions of the tale; and the fact that the monster never learns to speak is a great departure from the novel, in which he never shuts up.

Frankenstein became a box-office phenomenon, cuts notwithstanding, and it made Karloff the greatest horror star of the 1930s. His performance is brilliant, combining mime with pathos, a creature to be both feared and pitied. It set the standard for all the Frankenstein monsters to come.

As was the case with Browning's *Dracula*, the sets for *Frankenstein* were designed by Charles D. Hall, with the influence of German expressionism predominant. Winding staircases and looming towers dominate the bleak landscape, while the Strickfaden laboratory is replete with bubbling beakers, electrical coils, operating tables, and sparks flying every which way, all of which influenced just about every "mad doctor" film that came after. The movie's climax is somewhat marred by backdrops in which the seams literally show, as well as by an obvious dummy of Clive tossed by the monster from a windmill; yet Karloff's performance towers over the proceedings, making *Frankenstein* iconic and unforgettable.

Despite the tremendous box-office returns, it took Universal four years to mount a sequel to *Frankenstein*, but when it finally did arrive, it was a doozy. Whale would only return to his creation when he was assured he would have total control over the production, and he employed screenwriters William Hurlbut and John L. Balderston to come up with a new plot derived from a major event in Shelley's novel that the first film had ignored—the creation of a "bride" for the monster.

Originally announced in 1933 as *The Return of Frankenstein*, the sequel actually arrived in 1935 as *The Bride of Frankenstein*. The film turned out to be one of the greatest of all Universal horror movies. Colin Clive returned to the role of Henry Frankenstein, but this time he was assisted by his previous mentor Dr. Pretorious (Ernest Thesiger), a prissy alchemist who blackmails his former pupil into creating a mate for the monster, who, it turns out, has survived a fire in a windmill. All does not go according to plan, however, when the bride (Elsa Lanchester) takes one look at her groom (Karloff again) and screams her head off.

The Bride of Frankenstein had a bigger budget than its predecessor, and because Whale had total control, his eccentric sense of humor was at the forefront of the proceedings. Thesiger plays Pretorious as a preening homosexual (which eluded the censors), the monster sometimes appears Christ-like (there's a scene in which he's all but crucified when he's lashed to a pole by angry villagers), and odd, even bizarre characters abound. Whale managed to get all of this past the Hays Code, and the sequel is superior in just about every way to its original, a feat that is rarely accomplished in Hollywood. *The Bride of Frankenstein* became an enormous hit for Universal with both critics and audiences, and its reputation has only increased over the decades since.

Karloff played the monster one more time, in *Son of Frankenstein* (1939), directed by Rowland V. Lee, and the series continued throughout the 1940s with various actors appearing as the monster, including Lon Chaney Jr., Bela Lugosi (finally!), and Glenn Strange, ending with an out-and-out farce, 1948's *Abbott and Costello Meet Frankenstein*, in which the comedy duo of Bud Abbot and Lou Costello met up with Universal's classic monsters—Lugosi as Dracula, Chaney as the Wolf Man, and Glenn Strange as the monster—in a highly successful horror comedy that is still considered one of the best of its type today.

Wilder and Brooks loved these old films—especially those directed by Whale—and they wanted to spoof them, but with a great deal of affection. As Brooks later wrote, "Whale knew exactly how to scare the hell out of you, but he was also a great artist who was not appreciated for those talents as much as he should have been. We decided to base the look and spirit of *Young Frankenstein* on the James Whale classics."

Interviewed for the DVD of *Young Frankenstein*, Wilder recalled, "Why Frankenstein? Because when I was a little boy, I was scared to death of *Frankenstein*, the original one, and *Bride of Frankenstein*. I was also influenced by *Son of Frankenstein* and *Ghost of Frankenstein* . . . but mostly the biggest one was *Bride of Frankenstein*. I knew it was fertile ground to do a satire. But I also wanted it to end my way and not the way it did in the movie, and originally when I wrote it, I had Dr. Frankenstein being thrown off the precipice and the monster and my fiancée getting together."

Wilder remembered that the writing process was quite meticulous. "Mel and I met in my apartment in New York," he said in the DVD interview,

> for about two hours and 45 minutes on the first day to do with *Young Frankenstein*. And the first hour was spent with how to make the coffee, what kind of, what to have with the coffee . . . he had brought a bag of schnecken, which features prominently later on in the script. We talked about everything but the script. And after we'd had our talk about all the little nothings—which was sort of Mel's way of working, to slowly creep up on whatever you're going to do that's important, we start talking about the script; things from a to z, wild things that I knew in my heart weren't going to be in, but to touch all the bases.

Brooks and Wilder quickly got into the swing of things, finding a rhythm of working in tandem. Every night, after working on the editing of *Blazing Saddles*, Brooks would head to Wilder's hotel room, where the two of them concentrated on lovingly satirizing the James Whale oeuvre, and they quickly found they knew exactly where to go with the story. Wilder wrote in pencil on legal pads, which Brooks's secretary typed up the following day.

According to Wilder, Brooks taught him a most important lesson about screenwriting, that the first draft is simply the concept. Then, as

Brooks put it, "You take a sledgehammer and knock the pillars of the storyline as hard as you can. If they hold up, you keep it in. If they start to crumble, you have to rewrite, because the structure is everything."

Brooks and Wilder continued to hone their writing skills on *Young Frankenstein*, writing and rewriting until they were "more or less satisfied," according to Brooks. Along with parodying Whale's films, they returned to Shelley's original concepts for inspiration. Wilder and Brooks had each read Shelley's novel, so they had a good grasp of the book's themes: that the monster is misunderstood, a terribly deformed being who only wants to be loved and who has love in his heart for others. Although they were writing, as Brooks put it, "a crazy comedy," those themes were still present, as was the theme of a man playing God.

Casting the film crossed their minds before the screenplay was even half completed. It was decided from the very beginning that Wilder would play Dr. Frankenstein. The other big questions were these: who would play the monster, and who would play the strangely funny hunchback, Igor?

Actually, the character of Igor never appeared in either of Whale's films. Bela Lugosi played an oddly amusing character called Ygor in Lee's *Son of Frankenstein* in 1939, and the character became so popular that Lugosi played it again in the next movie in the series, *The Ghost of Frankenstein*, in 1942, despite the fact that Ygor had been killed off in *Son*. Iconic characters never stay dead for long in horror pictures.

The character of Igor in *Young Frankenstein* was really based on Fritz (Dwight Frye), Frankenstein's twisted, dwarfish assistant in the original *Frankenstein*. Fritz was one of Whale's true eccentrics, a bizarre oddball who paused on his way up the tower stairs to pull up his socks and who had a penchant for torturing the monster with a torch until the creature murdered him out of rage. Frye ended up playing a similar character called Karl in *The Bride of Frankenstein*, and in fact virtually built his career around playing such deformed and hunchbacked assistants to various mad doctors until his untimely death at age forty-four of a heart attack.

Wilder received a call one day during the screenwriting process from Mike Medavoy, Wilder's agent at that time; Medavoy would later become the head of Tri-Star Pictures. Medavoy had heard that Wilder and Brooks had been working on "that Frankenstein picture" and asked his client if there were any roles in it for Peter Boyle or Marty Feldman. Wilder was curious as to why Medavoy was pitching them, to which he replied that he was not only Wilder's agent, he was now representing Boyle and Feldman.

According to Wilder, he had recently seen a TV show called *The Marty Feldman Comedy Machine*, a summer replacement series that was coproduced by ATV in the UK and ABC TV in the United States. It had starred the pop-eyed British comic and had opening and closing credits animated and designed by Terry Gilliam of *Monty Python's Flying Circus*. Its madcap, anarchic humor had appealed to Wilder. The night he received the phone call from Medavoy, he wrote the scene in which Frederick Frankenstein and Igor meet for the first time at Transylvania Station, while picturing himself in the role of Frederick and Feldman as Igor. He sent his four typewritten pages to Medavoy, who called him two days later to tell him that he felt he could sell the concept. And he immediately thought of Brooks to direct it—which, of course, had already occurred to Wilder.

And so a monster came to be born—well, eventually.

8

"THERE WOLF, THERE CASTLE"

In the introduction to his book *Young Frankenstein: The Story of the Making of the Film*, Brooks wrote, "You have to really know a genre to make fun of it, and to really know it, you have to love it. . . . I was five years old in 1931 when James Whale's *Frankenstein* came out. The following summer the movie played in Williamsburg and my older brother, Bernie, took me to see it[;] . . . and that movie scared the hell out of me."

At the top of the page of his *Young Frankenstein* concept, Wilder wrote, "In black and white." He wasn't certain that any studio would greenlight a black-and-white movie at that time in film history; most of them insisted on color. This was essentially due to television revenues for feature films. American TV had gone all-color in 1966, and nearly all features made since that year were in color. There were a few exceptions, however. Director Peter Bogdanovich had filmed his Oscar-winning *The Last Picture Show* (1971) in black and white for "artistic" reasons, while horrormeister George A. Romero had shot his *Night of the Living Dead* (1968) in monochrome for budgetary reasons. More recently, Bogdanovich had also lensed *Paper Moon* (1973) in black and white, which, coincidentally, featured Madeline Kahn along with Ryan O'Neal and his daughter Tatum. The black-and-white cinematography of those films seemed to enhance rather than detract from their box office and critical success, and so black and white was, to a certain extent, "in" again.

In any case, Wilder felt confident that Brooks would be able to shoot the movie in black and white—as an homage to the old Universal pictures—if he fought hard enough for it. While he was writing the story, Wilder felt that they needed a "really frightening" woman to open the door of Frankenstein's castle, letting in Dr. Frankenstein— preferably in a thunderstorm. The female character who had scared Wilder the most in movies he had seen in his youth had been Mrs. Danvers (Judith Anderson) in Alfred Hitchcock's *Rebecca* (1940). He also needed an appropriately unusual name for his forbidding female, so he consulted a book of letters from and to Sigmund Freud that he just happened to have on hand. He discovered that someone named Blucher had written to Freud, a word that allegedly meant "glue" in German. At the time, he didn't know the meaning, but he felt somehow that the mere utterance of her name would frighten horses. Once he discovered what "blucher" actually meant, it made even more sense, as glue was made from—well, let's not go there.

After he finished the first fifty-eight pages of the script—about half of it—he flew to Los Angeles and showed the pages to Brooks. All Brooks said was, "Okay, now let's talk about what happens next." Wilder assumed that meant that Brooks liked what he had written so far.

When he returned to New York, Wilder started writing the second half. As it happened, Brooks was in total agreement with Wilder that the film needed to be in black and white to salute the old Universal horror films. They felt that they needed a budget of at least $2 million dollars.

Producer Michael Gruskoff had just made a sci-fi movie called *Silent Running* (1972), starring Bruce Dern and directed by Douglas Trumbull; the movie had not been a huge box-office hit, but it had achieved some critical acclaim. A former agent, Gruskoff had worked with Brooks at the William Morris Agency, so they had a good relationship. Gruskoff agreed to produce *Young Frankenstein*, with Brooks directing and Wilder starring, and the three men went to Columbia Pictures to pitch the script.

I've never understood why Brooks and company didn't take the project to Universal from the get-go. It would have made perfect sense; the company's history with the genre, and with Frankenstein in particular, was world renowned. And they could have used the original Jack Pierce makeup, which was copyrighted by Universal, for the monster. For whatever reason, though, they took it to Columbia, and it didn't work out very well.

It's important to remember that when they went to Columbia, *Blazing Saddles* had not yet been released. Brooks's reputation as a money-making director/producer was not yet established. Nevertheless, Columbia liked the script, and they offered $1.5 million dollars to produce it. Brooks, Gruskoff, and Wilder had already discussed the budget, and they felt they couldn't make the film they wanted to make for under $2 million. Gruskoff haggled and got Columbia to agree to

Madeline Kahn as Lili Von Shtüpp and Cleavon Little as Sheriff Bart get to know each other. WARNER BROS./ PHOTOFEST © WARNER BROS.

Sheriff Bart (Cleavon Little) and the Waco Kid (Gene Wilder).
WARNER BROS./PHOTOFEST © WARNER BROS.

Harvey Korman as Hedley (not Hedy) Lamarr. WARNER BROS./PHOTOFEST © WARNER BROS.

Cleavon Little as Sheriff
Bart and Gene Wilder
as the Waco Kid.

Gene Wilder as the
Waco Kid.

Madeline Kahn as Lili Von Shtüpp.

Original Poster designed by Anthony Goldschmidt and John Alvin. WARNER BROS./
PHOTOFEST © WARNER BROS.

Slim Pickens as Taggart and Alex Karras as the rather dim Mongo. WARNER BROS./
PHOTOFEST © WARNER BROS.

Hedley Lamarr (Harvey Korman) and Lili Von Shtüpp (Madeline Kahn) have a tete-a-tete.
WARNER BROS./PHOTOFEST © WARNER BROS.

Gene Wilder (The Waco Kid) and Cleavon Little (Sheriff Bart). WARNER BROS./PHOTOFEST © WARNER BROS.

Mel Brooks as the rather Yiddish Indian Chief. WARNER BROS./PHOTOFEST © WARNER BROS.

Mel Brooks as Governor Lepetomane and Robyn Hilton as his, um, secretary. WARNER BROS./PHOTOFEST © WARNER BROS.

Marty Feldman as Igor. 20TH CENTURY FOX/PHOTOFEST ©TWENTIETH CENTURY FOX FILM CORPORATION

Mel Brooks and Gene Wilder behind the scenes. 20TH CENTURY FOX/PHOTOFEST ©TWENTIETH CENTURY FOX FILM CORPORATION

Madeline Kahn as Elizabeth, a.k.a. The Bride. 20TH CENTURY FOX/PHOTOFEST ©TWENTIETH CENTURY FOX FILM CORPORATION

The original poster designed by Anthony Goldschmidt and John Alvin. 20TH CENTURY FOX/PHOTOFEST ©TWENTIETH CENTURY FOX FILM CORPORATION

Kenneth Mars as Inspector Kemp, complete with wooden arm. 20TH CENTURY FOX/PHOTOFEST ©TWENTIETH CENTURY FOX FILM CORPORATION

Madeline Kahn (Elizabeth) and Peter Boyle (the monster) in a tender moment. 20TH CENTURY FOX/PHOTOFEST ©TWENTIETH CENTURY FOX FILM CORPORATION

Gene Hackman as the blind man, a character featured in the original Mary Shelley novel. 20TH CENTURY FOX/ PHOTOFEST ©TWENTIETH CENTURY FOX FILM CORPORATION

Marty Feldman and "Abby Normal." 20TH CENTURY FOX/PHOTOFEST ©TWENTIETH CENTURY
FOX FILM CORPORATION

Mel Brooks and Peter Boyle on set.
20TH CENTURY FOX/PHOTOFEST ©TWENTIETH
CENTURY FOX FILM CORPORATION

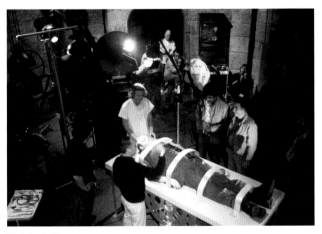

Behind the scenes. 20TH CENTURY FOX/PHOTOFEST
©TWENTIETH CENTURY FOX FILM CORPORATION

L–R: Mel Brooks, Peter Boyle, Teri Garr, Gene Wilder, Cloris Leachman relaxing. 20TH CENTURY FOX/ PHOTOFEST ©TWENTIETH CENTURY FOX FILM CORPORATION

L–R: Teri Garr, Gene Wilder, Marty Feldman, Peter Boyle, Mel Brooks on the set. 20TH CENTURY FOX/PHOTOFEST ©TWENTIETH CENTURY FOX FILM CORPORATION

L–R: Cloris Leachman, Teri Garr, Mel Brooks, Marty Feldman, Unidentified. 20TH CENTURY FOX/PHOTOFEST ©TWENTIETH CENTURY FOX FILM CORPORATION

$1.75 million. Everybody shook hands. It was a deal. Except that it wasn't.

Brooks turned when he reached the office door and said, "Oh, by the way, we're going to make it in black and white." Then he walked out the door.

As Brooks later wrote, "a thundering herd of studio executives" chased them down the hallway. They seemed horrified. "No black and white!" they screamed. Brooks insisted one of them said, "Peru just got color! Everything is in color! Nobody makes black-and-white movies anymore!" Apparently, the executives thought that movies like *The Last Picture Show* were just flukes.

As Brooks wrote, "The thing about satire is the walls, the floors, the costumes, everything surrounding the comedy has to be real. If we were going to satirize the classic 1930s Universal Frankenstein pictures, our film had to be in black and white."

The Columbia execs, headed by John Veitch, executive director of the meeting, tried to play a little Hollywood-type trick on Brooks. They offered him a compromise: shoot it in color, and they'd diffuse it and desaturate it for the American market, but the rest of the world would see it in color. Brooks knew they were pulling his leg; as he put it, "[s]tudios have a way of promising the world and giving you zero." Brooks nixed the idea, because he knew that they'd release it in color in the United States anyway; they needed those television residuals, after all.

Brooks got technical with them, throwing them off the track. He pointed out that there was a German film stock called Agfa, a rich, true black-and-white type of stock. That was the only film stock he was willing to use on *Young Frankenstein*. The Columbia bigwigs balked.

If he insisted on shooting on black-and-white film stock, that would break the deal.

Gruskoff, Brooks, and Wilder all agreed: "Then break it!"

One of the ironies is that over twenty years later—in 1994, to be exact—Veitch was one of the producers, along with Francis Ford Coppola, of *Mary Shelley's Frankenstein*, directed by and starring Kenneth Branagh, with Robert DeNiro as the creature. This serious approach to the story was not a huge box-office success, so it wasn't much of a consolation prize for Veitch.

That same day after the meeting, Gruskoff pointed out to Brooks that his friend "Laddie"—the nickname for Alan Ladd Jr., son of the iconic movie star of such films as *This Gun for Hire* (1942) and *Shane* (1953)—had just been appointed vice president of creative affairs at 20th Century Fox. Ladd and Gruskoff had been agents together and were still good friends. With Brooks's and Wilder's approval, Gruskoff dropped off a copy of the *Young Frankenstein* script to Ladd's house that night.

Ladd read the script—twice!—between 11:00 p.m. and 1:00 a.m., so enchanted by it that he couldn't put it down, according to Brooks. When Brooks met with Ladd soon afterward, he was impressed by the fact that the new Fox executive agreed that it should be produced in black and white. Brooks later wrote, "I knew right then and there that I had finally met a studio chief that I could really trust."

Ladd was quoted in *Young Frankenstein: The Story of the Making of the Film*: "Mel said, 'I want it to be in black and white.' And I said, 'That's all right, all the old horror films were in black and white.' It made sense to me. But I did worry about the black and white. A lot of theater owners wouldn't take a movie unless it was in color. The truth is I was worried about it, but I didn't tell them that. And we made the deal."

Ladd approved a budget of $2.4 million—more than Brooks, Wilder, and Gruskoff had asked for—and this was before *Blazing Saddles* had become the blockbuster hit it became. It was the beginning of a beautiful friendship between Brooks and Fox, who later signed a three-picture deal with the company and who remained one of Ladd's best friends until the latter's death in 2022.

Once casting began, so did the fun. Brooks once again cast Kenneth Mars, who had played the off-the-wall German playwright of *Springtime for Hitler* in *The Producers*, as the equally mad German Inspector Kemp in *Young Frankenstein*. The character was based on Inspector Krogh (Lionel Atwill) in *Son of Frankenstein*, who had once had his arm torn out by the roots by the Frankenstein monster (Karloff). As Brooks and Wilder revamped the character, in addition to a wooden arm, he also wore a black eyepatch over one eye. To make things as silly as possible, Brooks suggested that he wear a monocle over his eyepatch, which of course would have been utterly useless.

Mars was in Buffalo, New York, doing a play that winter when Brooks called him backstage before the curtain went up. Mars said later that Brooks asked him what he was doing in Buffalo, and Mars replied that "Nome was too warm." Then Brooks told him about the role and asked him if, on top of his eyepatch, he'd be willing to wear a monocle. "Is that too much?" Brooks asked. Mars replied that, no, it wasn't too much, and Brooks told him he had the part.

For the part of Frau Blucher, the truly odd housekeeper of the castle, Brooks cast the highly talented Cloris Leachman, who had recently won a Best Supporting Actress Oscar for her turn in *The Last Picture*

Show. Born in Des Moines, Iowa, in 1926, Leachman had been knocking about the business for quite some time, most notably in such films as Robert Aldrich's *Kiss Me Deadly* (1956), *The Rack* that same year, and *Butch Cassidy and the Sundance Kid* (1969). She was also ubiquitous on television in episodes of such classic series as *The Twilight Zone*, *Gunsmoke*, and *Alfred Hitchcock Presents*. She was also a regular on *The Mary Tyler Moore Show*, for which she won an Emmy.

Leachman later said that she thought the script was "wonderful," but she was concerned about the role because she had never done a German accent before. She asked a number of people if they knew how to do one. Luckily, Brooks's mother happened to be on the set one day, and she knew both German and Yiddish. She assisted Leachman with her accent, which turned out to be one of the funniest parts of the film.

"Frau Blucher was a good part," Wilder said in an interview for the DVD of *Young Frankenstein*. "A crazy lady. But when Cloris Leachman brought the reality to it, she was tutti fruitti. I wanted the audience to know that, even though they don't know why yet, the horses know that this is a terrifying woman and God knows what she's done to them when no one's watching."

Pre-casting had included Wilder in the title role, Feldman as Igor—and Peter Boyle as the monster. Brooks had seen Boyle in the movie *Joe* (1970)—a political drama that was hardly comedic—and thought he gave a terrific performance. Brooks knew that an actor was an actor, and if he could do drama, he could do comedy. Boyle proved his range in such subsequent films as *The Candidate* (1972), *Steelyard Blues*, and *The Friends of Eddie Coyle* (both 1973); and Brooks wanted him for his monster. The character of Joe in his breakout movie proved to Brooks that Boyle had the acting chops needed to play the monster: in *Joe*,

Boyle alternated between scary and sweet, and the monster had to be both.

"The monster worked great on paper," Wilder said in a later interview,

> but we didn't know if it would work until Peter walked in. I don't know how many people have seen Peter in real life, but he is so childlike, so innocent; you know, he doesn't say words for about an hour, but he started doing things (making hand gestures). The catching butterflies thing was his idea. To catch butterflies, it brought the part to life. I think this cast was blessed in a way; I don't say blessed by God, but blessed by something, because everyone found themselves.

During casting, Brooks saw a number of actresses for the role of Inga, Dr. Frankenstein's lab assistant, finally settling on the lovely, talented, and funny Teri Garr. Born in 1944, Garr had been in the business for a while before she got her first real acting break in a 1968 episode of *Star Trek* titled *Assignment: Earth*. From that point on, she found herself in demand for mostly comedic roles in such films as *Head* (1968), *Changes* (1969), and *The Moonshine War* (1970), before garnering serious attention in Francis Ford Coppola's *The Conversation* (1974), the film she appeared in opposite Gene Hackman just prior to *Young Frankenstein*.

Garr had originally auditioned for the role of Elizabeth, while Madeline Kahn had originally tried out for the role of Inga. After giving it some thought, though, Kahn decided she would rather play Elizabeth, leaving Brooks to recast the role of Inga. He told Garr that if she could come back the next day and impress him with her German accent, he would give her the role.

During her audition, Brooks was delighted with Garr's "unique" German accent. When she read the line during which Frau Blucher removes the steel restraints from the monster, who is lying on the lab table, Garr's line as scripted was "No, no, you musn't!" The way Garr read it, however, in her faux German accent was, "No, no, you *mozzn't!*" Brooks cracked up and she got the part. Garr has said in interviews that she based the accent on that of Cher's wigmaker, with whom she worked on *The Sonny and Cher Comedy Hour* in 1971.

Having mastered the accent, Garr realized after she read the part that "it was all about boobs." She was not about to let the fact that she was rather lacking in that department keep her from securing the role. She made sure that she wore a fuzzy pink sweater and a large padded bra stuffed with socks for her second audition—and she got the part.

Completing the trio of funny ladies in *Young Frankenstein* was the ever-reliable Kahn, returning from her comedic triumph in *Blazing Saddles*. Brooks and Wilder had written the role of Elizabeth as a kind of upper-class dame who was more interested in diamonds than in reanimating dead tissue, and he knew that Kahn could knock that kind of role out of the park.

In an interview for the DVD of *Young Frankenstein*, Wilder recalled, "Madeline didn't want to play the lab assistant, she wanted to play the fiancée. I thought she must be nuts because I thought the lab assistant was a much better part. Well, it was, until Madeline put her own stamp on the fiancée."

It was Brooks's idea to have Elizabeth engage in a love scene with the monster in which, instead of screaming, she bursts into song: "Oh, sweet mystery of life, at last I've found you," she sings, and obviously Kahn could pull that off as well. Then, for the pièce de résistance toward the end of the film, Brooks and Wilder modeled her hair style after Elsa Lanchester's in *The Bride of Frankenstein*—comic genius, no doubt about it.

One of the most delightful casting choices of *Young Frankenstein* turned out to be the actor who played the blind hermit, portrayed in the original *Bride of Frankenstein* by character actor O. P. Heggie. By a fortuitous coincidence, Wilder played tennis every Saturday with none other than Gene Hackman. During one of their tennis matches, Hackman asked Wilder what project he was currently working on, and Wilder told him a bit about *Young Frankenstein*. After starring in such heavy dramatic films as *The French Connection* (1971) and *The Conversation* (1974), Hackman was eager to lighten up his image, and he immediately asked Wilder if there might be a role in *Young Frankenstein* for him.

Wilder, thinking this might be too good to be true, calmly said, "Yes, there is," and he told Hackman about the role of the old blind hermit. He pointed out that it was merely a cameo and started to apologize for it, but Hackman interrupted and said, "It sounds perfect! Count me in!"

In a later interview, Wilder said, "Now Gene Hackman asked me privately, because I knew him, 'Is there some little part I could play?' He meant, like the second officer or something, you know, just to walk through, say a line and go out. I said, 'Well, I'll talk to Mel and we'll see.' And I talked to Mel and we agreed there was only one part and that was the blind man."

When Wilder told Brooks about Hackman's interest, Brooks was thrilled. An Oscar-winning actor in a cameo? What could be better? Hackman was cast as the hermit and didn't take a penny for it. He did it as a favor and received minor billing as "Blind Man" in the movie. Makeup master William Tuttle created the character's beard, which was so realistic Hackman was difficult to recognize. Tuttle also created the chin mole for Leachman and the rather icky mummified corpse of Beaufort Frankenstein seen in the film's opening.

Although it was Wilder's idea, he and Brooks had agreed at the outset that Brooks would not act in *Young Frankenstein*; Wilder didn't want Brooks to dilute his concentration on directing by playing one of his usual small roles.

Supporting actors in the cast included the venerable Richard Haydn (*The Sound of Music*, 1965) as Herr Falkstein, Liam Dunn from *Blazing Saddles* as Mr. Hilltop, Danny Goldman (Robert Altman's *M*A*S*H*, 1970) as a medical student, Oscar Beregi Jr. (*Everything You Always Wanted to Know About Sex . . .*) as a sadistic jailer, veteran character actor Arthur Malet (*Mary Poppins*, 1964) as a village elder, former producer Richard A. Roth (*Summer of '42*, 1971) as Inspector Kemp's assistant, Monte Landis (*Myra Breckinridge*, 1970), and Rusty Blitz (*The Producers*) as gravediggers, Anne Beesley (*The Memory of Us*, 1974) as the little girl and John Madison (*Young Goodman Brown*, 1972) as a villager.

Casting, of course, was only one of the challenges in bringing *Young Frankenstein* to life. There was another hump to leap over.

9

"WHAT HUMP?"

For Brooks and Wilder, the look of *Young Frankenstein* was all-important. Veteran cinematographer Gerald Hirschfeld was chosen to photograph the film. Hirschfeld had been in the business since the 1940s, with his first film as cinematographer being *Shades of Gray* (1948), a short about neuropsychiatric cases during World War II. More recently, he had photographed *Fail Safe* (1964)—something of a black-and-white masterpiece—as well as the color films *Goodbye Columbus* (1969) and *Diary of a Mad Housewife* (1970).

Hirschfeld had never worked with Brooks before, and at first he was a bit put off in his interview with the director by Brooks's pointing out what he called "mistakes" in the cinematography of *Diary of a Mad Housewife*. Brooks thought that perhaps the white tub in the bathroom in that film was too bright, and that the gels "shimmered" too much in the bedroom scene. Hirschfeld later said in an interview, "At first I took him seriously and was more than a little upset, until I realized he was doing his 'thing' and pulling my leg, because there was no tub and the bedroom was an interior set that didn't require window gels. So I pulled his leg and said, 'One more derogatory remark about my work and I'll leave.' We understood each other and laughed."

In an article he wrote called "The Story behind the Filming of *Young Frankenstein*" for *American Cinematographer* that was published shortly before the release of the film, Hirschfeld recalled, "At first, I balked at the decision to do the film in black and white, suggesting that we start in black and white, as the film opens in old-time Transylvania, and then segue to color as we go to modern-day Baltimore to meet young Dr. Frankenstein. But the director was firm, and I soon realized, as I progressed more into the feeling of the film, that he was 100% correct."

Another important behind-the-scenes contributor to the look of *Young Frankenstein* was a gentleman by the name of Kenneth Strickfaden. Beginning with his electrical special effects on James Whale's *Frankenstein*, Strickfaden became Hollywood's go-to guy for practical special effects, electrical props, and set design. He created the scientific apparatus for over a hundred films, ranging from Whale's first two *Frankenstein* films to *The Mask of Fu Manchu* (1932, also starring Karloff) to *The Wizard of Oz* (1939). Brooks was thrilled to discover that not only was Strickfaden still alive (he was born in 1896), he was still in the film business, having recently provided the "mad lab" equipment for the schlocky *Dracula vs. Frankenstein* (1971) and the even schlockier *Blackenstein* (1973). Still living in the Los Angeles area, Strickfaden had even supplied the lab equipment for the TV series *The Munsters* (1964–1966)—itself a takeoff on the old Universal horror films.

Brooks's production manager, Frank Bauer, contacted Strickfaden and found that he had stored the original equipment for the Frankenstein films in his garage in Santa Monica. An electrician by trade, Strickfaden was only too happy to throw the switch for Brooks to demonstrate that, after over forty years, his original buzzing, whirring, crackling lab equipment from *Frankenstein* still worked. Brooks offered him a deal whereby he would rent the equipment—Strickfaden was asking only $1,000 for it, but Brooks offered him $2,500—and gave Strickfaden the screen credit that he had never received on the original films. Strickfaden was very amenable to being part of the production, which, ironically, turned out to be his last film. He passed away ten years later, in 1984, at the age of eighty-seven.

In 1974, Strickfaden was interviewed by the *Los Angeles Times* to promote the film. He related, "Most of the [laboratory pieces] are remnants of the original equipment and some are copies. Some have been altered and quite a few of them burned up in the intervening years."

Strickfaden went on to say that the cast and crew were "so nice. They treat me like the old man that I am. Still, I put in a good day's work. I only watch the action when my equipment is in use. . . . Brooks really knows what he's doing. He's after lots of comedy but doesn't want to lose the melodrama. His comedy for this is like a good Rembrandt—just a little dash of color in with the primary colors."

Not only was Strickfaden on the set during the laboratory scenes, he also created some new electrical devices just for *Young Frankenstein*. Hirschfeld recalled, "The laboratory was ablaze at times with 'Jacob's Ladders,' which are spark-gaps that climbed two V-shaped electrodes until the spark finally escapes at the top in a six-inch span of lightning. The 'Melodic Melinda,' a humorously named gadget, created arcs that jumped from contact to contact in prescribed rhythm, from waltz time to jazz tempos!"

The makeup for the monster was all-important, of course, and Brooks hired brilliant veteran makeup creator William Tuttle for the job. Tuttle had worked at MGM for many years, supervising makeup on such films as *The Wizard of Oz* (1939) and *The Time Machine* (1960). He also supplied the makeup effects for numerous episodes of *The Twilight Zone* between 1959 and 1964, including for the memorable episodes *Eye of the Beholder* and *Nightmare at 20,000 Feet*. In 1965, Tuttle received a special Oscar for his extraordinary work on *7 Faces of Dr. Lao*, released the previous year, in which he transferred actor Tony Randall into, among other things, Merlin, Medusa, Pan, and the Abominable Snowman.

When Brooks told Tuttle that *Young Frankenstein* would be in black and white, Tuttle hugged him. He pointed out to Brooks that if the film had been made in color, the monster's face would look blue-green. In black and white, however, the makeup would look "incredible," according to Tuttle.

As with the original films with Karloff, greenish makeup was applied to Boyle's face, which not only made his features more prominent but had a grayish look in black and white. Although the original iconic makeup couldn't be used because of copyright reasons, Tuttle's vision parodied the Pierce/Karloff look, but instead of bolts in the monster's neck, there was a zipper.

In a later interview, Tuttle said that the zipper in the neck was Brooks's idea. "I have to give him credit for that," he said. He recalled that Brooks asked him if he could have the zipper in the neck, as (1) it was funny and (2) it was a good way around the copyrighted Pierce/Karloff makeup. So Tuttle gave him a zipper. "It's a real zipper, too," he noted proudly.

During preproduction, Tuttle showed Brooks several versions of the monster's face. Brooks instructed him to give the face a character that was "dangerous looking, but at times he should also be beautiful and angelic."

Hirschfeld also worked closely with Tuttle, attempting to find the correct way to photograph the monster's makeup. Hirschfeld later wrote,

> The green color, in black and white, gave the skin a "dead" look; it worked fine. However, my problem was that the film was more sensitive to that green color than to normal flesh tones. The monster always required a lower-intensity key light to bring him into balance with the other players, or he had to be netted down by a moving net guided by the key-grip. Since all good monsters have larger than normal frontal lobes, ours was no exception. In order to bring out the protruberances and throw the eyes into mysterious shadows, the monster's key light was kept very high, often hanging from the ceiling—not easy to do, but the look was right.

As *Young Frankenstein* is essentially a period piece—we're never told exactly when it takes place, but it seems to be the 1930s—costumes were also important. Again, Brooks went straight to the top, employing the services of veteran costume designer Dorothy Jeakins, who had worked with such great Hollywood directors as Cecil B. DeMille, William Wyler, and John Huston. Among other actresses, Jeakins had clothed Marilyn Monroe in *Niagara* (1953), Jean Simmons in *Elmer Gantry* (1960), and Barbra Streisand in *The Way We Were* (1973). Jeakins won three Oscars, for *Joan of Arc* (1948, which she shared with Barbara Karinska), *Samson and Delilah* (1949, which she shared with Edith Head), and *Night of the Iguana* (1964), which she won on her own. Jeakins was a specialist in period costumes, having designed them for such films as *Les Miserables* (1952), *Titanic* (1953), and *The Sound of Music* (1965), among many other costume pictures.

According to Brooks, Jeakins was one of the best costume designers to ever work in Hollywood, and when he met with her, she asked him what he wanted. Did he want Alsatian costumes for the villagers? German, Bavarian, Transylvanian? Brooks realized he was out of his depth. He told her that she was the expert, so it was up to her. Most of the costumes ended up looking Bavarian, à la the old Universal movies.

Interestingly enough, the wardrobe mistress on *Young Frankenstein* was Phyllis Lind Garr, Teri Garr's mother. This wasn't just a case of nepotism: Teri's mom had worked on such films as *The Graduate* (1967), *Frogs* (1972), and *Dirty Mary Crazy Larry* (1973); and she was costume designer on fifty-two episodes of TV's *That Girl* from 1966 through 1968.

James Whale's original *Frankenstein* had featured no musical score, as was the case with most early talkies. *Bride of Frankenstein* featured a splendid Franz Waxman score, while *Son of Frankenstein* was memorably scored by Frank Skinner, who lent his talents to many of the classic Universal horrors. Composer John Morris had already scored *Blazing Saddles*, so Brooks brought him back for *Young Frankenstein*, giving him instructions to compose a score that harked back to the classic compositions of Waxman and Skinner.

Brooks told Morris that he didn't really want "scary music," as that had nothing to do with the main characters. His instructions to Morris were to write the most beautiful eastern European lullaby he could come up with, and that theme would become "the heart of the monster." By this time, Morris and Brooks understood each other well, and the composer gave him something that would capture the emotional core of the movie.

Stage 5 at Fox was to be the center of operations, where all the castle interiors would be shot. It was a huge facility and had all the space they needed. Brooks hired Dale Hennesy, who had recently worked on Don Siegel's *Dirty Harry* (1971) as his production designer. Hennesy's parents had both been designers and layout artists for Walt Disney, and he had begun working at Fox as an illustrator. He moved quickly up the ladder after doing illustration work on *The King and I* (1956) and *South Pacific* (1958), becoming art director on *Flower Drum Song* (1961). Moving from musicals to sci-fi, Hennesy won an Academy Award for Best Art Direction for *Fantastic Voyage* (1966), and from there went from strength to strength on such films as *In Like Flint* (1967), *Slither*, and *Battle for the Planet of the Apes* (both 1973). He moved back and forth between art direction and production design, beginning with the latter in 1963 for *Under the Yum-Yum Tree* and going on to do production design for such high-profile movies as Woody Allen's *Everything You Always Wanted to Know About Sex . . .* and *Sleeper* (both 1972).

Hennesy's budget for the sets was $400,000 and he made the most of it: "sets, cobbled streets and assembled rooms of a type that would make any cinematographer's mouth water," as Hirschfeld put it. Hennesy had the rooms decorated in varying degrees of gray stone, which Hirschfeld could reproduce in any tone he chose, depending on the amount of light he put on them and ultimately controlled by the increase in contrast due to the film processing used.

Hennesy created a vast complex of castle courtyards, reception hall, winding spiral staircases, secret passageways, rooms with secret rotating panels, and a laboratory with an operating table that was elevated through the roof with steel chains onto a detailed rooftop set surrounded by a cloudy, atmospherically stormy backdrop. They were sets that would have made James Whale's art director on the 1931 *Frankenstein*, Charles D. Hall, pleased as punch.

Hennesy's castle looks damp, "as if it were made of sweating stone," according to Brooks, and at fifteen thousand square feet and thirty-five feet high, was an enormous interior set. The laboratory was just as immense, if not larger, than the lab sets for the original *Frankenstein* and *Bride of Frankenstein*, and just as full of oddball props, thanks to Strickfaden and set decorator Robert De Vestel, who decorated the lab with test tubes from the early twentieth century, Bunsen burners, and beakers, while filling the other rooms in the castle with period drapes, chandeliers, candelabras, stone stairs, tapestries, plates made of pewter, goblets, and stone floors. They were sets that would have made James Whale beam.

As if that weren't enough, outdoor locations for the movie were to be filmed at MGM Studios, who weren't making many movies at the time but were more than happy to rent out their facilities to filmmakers. The MGM back lot was used for two big exterior scenes, the graveyard where Frankenstein and Igor dig up a body, and the Bavarian village full of cobblestone streets and quaint houses.

Brooks was lucky to secure the MGM lot for his village, as the studio had a complete Bavarian village set complete with all the trimmings. As they were doing a period movie, Brooks wanted artisans who had knowledge of how those films looked and who, perhaps, had actually worked on some of them.

It was all quite Transylvanian. Well, the Universal style of Transylvania in any case, which seemed more Bavarian than anything else. But that was the point: to recreate the look and feel of the old Universal monster movies, not to be geographically accurate.

Brooks hired John Monte as set photographer. The job of a set photographer was to take still photos of the sets, sometimes featuring the actors and sometimes just highlighting the sets themselves. Monte had been set photographer on such films as *Guess Who's Coming to Dinner?* (1967) and *The New Centurions* (1972), so he knew his way around movie sets. Brooks liked the fact that Monte was good at his job and never interfered with the production going on around him. He was very pleased with Monte's work, which helped a great deal in publicizing the film.

The unit publicist was John Campbell, a Hollywood veteran whose experience went back to 1955 on *House of Bamboo*, a crime drama starring Robert Ryan, Robert Stack, and Shirley Yamaguchi, and who also worked on such high-profile movies as *The Poseidon Adventure* (1972) and *Battle for the Planet of the Apes* (1973). Campbell had also worked with the likes of John Ford and John Huston in various capacities, and he told journalist Loraine Alterman on the set that he had never seen a director do as many takes as Brooks. He assumed that it was to get the comic timing just right. And indeed, Alterman noted, the scene she witnessed being filmed (the sequence with the gravediggers, played by Monte Landis and Rusty Blitz) lasted less than a minute of screen time, but Brooks spent a couple of hours to get it just right.

The mad doctors and their assistants were all assembled. Now it was time to create a monster.

10

"WALK THIS WAY"

Principal photography commenced on *Young Frankenstein* on February 19, 1974—a little over a week after *Blazing Saddles* opened nationwide—and anyone who has seen the outtakes featuring Wilder, Feldman, Garr, and the others will know that one of Brooks's biggest on-set problems was getting his cast to keep a straight face. To hear him tell it, filming *Young Frankenstein* was almost nonstop hilarity, with the cast having as much fun as the audience eventually would. There was a lot of improvisation; for example, the recurring bit that has Igor switching which side of his back his hump was on was an invention of Feldman's. The mischievous actor had been shifting his hump back and forth for several days before the other actors—and Brooks—noticed it. When they did, it was decided to add it to the script—and when Frederick asks him, "Wasn't your hump on the other side?" Igor replies, "What hump?"

Gene Hackman ad-libbed his line "I was gonna make espresso." That scene, after the monster has run out of the hermit's cabin, immediately fades to black, in part because the cast and crew erupted into fits of laughter after Hackman's ad-lib. Hackman was unable to repeat the line without laughing along with everyone else, so the first take was used.

Cloris Leachman also had fun ad-libbing her lines about offering "varm milk" and "Ovaltine" to Frederick. In a later scene, when Frederick leans in to kiss Elizabeth goodnight in her bedroom, Madeline Kahn ad-libbed her quip, "No tongues."

Kahn later claimed that she came up with the choice of singing "Ah! Sweet Mystery of Life." According to her, Brooks wanted her character to burst into song when the monster ravished her, but in the script he specified the Irving Berlin song, "Cheek to Cheek," which began with the line, "Heaven, I'm in Heaven." Kahn tried to make that work, but she had difficulty with it. She wanted something that started with "Ah!" or "Oh!" so that it sounded as if she were starting to scream. She asked Mel if she could try "Ah! Sweet Mystery of Life," and he gave her the go-ahead. The rest is cinematic history.

The idea of Frederick's dart hitting a cat during his game with Inspector Kemp was also ad-libbed on the set. When Wilder threw his dart off-camera, Brooks screamed like an injured cat and everyone thought that was quite funny, so it stayed in the film. Wilder constantly cracked up, ruining several takes. Leachman later recalled, "He killed every take [with his laughter] and nothing was done about it!" Brooks would have to call for as many as fifteen takes before Wilder could regain his composure.

According to Brooks, the scene that required the most takes was the one in which Igor growls at and bites Elizabeth's fur wrap. The reason for so many takes—in addition to the fact that Feldman was just naturally hilarious as Igor—was because every time he bit the wrap, he ended up with a piece of fur in his mouth that he couldn't shake.

Everyone on the set cracked up, a lot of film was used, and a lot of money was spent—but it was all worth it.

Alterman was on the set for the filming of that sequence, and she reported it in her usual detail: Kahn was driven onto the set in a 1920 limousine and Brooks got a bit exasperated with the limo driver because he drove the car just a bit too fast and it made too much noise. Ultimately, the driver slowed down and drove in nearly silently, but then, in retrieving Kahn's luggage, he bumped the bags down too hard on the cobblestones, which interfered with the dialogue. On the next take, one of the crew placed a furniture pad on the stones to muffle the noise.

Once that part of the scene was in the can, Brooks commenced working on the scene in which the "bit" between Feldman and Kahn took place. While Wilder welcomed her, Feldman bit the fox boa and growled like a dog, followed by Kahn hitting him on the head with her purse.

Wilder pointed out that they were suddenly turning into the Marx Brothers. Brooks thought that was a great idea and encouraged them to be more "Marxist." Every time they attempted to get through the line, everyone—including the crew—cracked up at Feldman's perfect Groucho imitation. "To Hell with the public," Brooks finally said, through tears of laughter. "We had our laugh."

The next two takes went smoothly according to Alterman, although Brooks was biting his forearm and shaking with silent laughter during each one. Brooks wasn't entirely satisfied with Wilder's line delivery, however, and instructed him on exactly how to say, "Igor, would you give me a hand with the bags?" After Brooks cried, "Action!" Wilder suddenly burst into hysterical laughter. Kahn and Teri quickly followed suit and Feldman collapsed onto the luggage. Brooks wondered if they'd ever get the timing right.

Wilder pointed out to Brooks that what sent him over the edge was Feldman biting off the foot of the fox boa; he said that he was prepared to deliver his line when he saw that Feldman had the foot in his mouth "and it wasn't attached to anything."

At that point, Feldman became concerned that the fox boa might have been a real fox; it turned out that Feldman had been a vegetarian for most of his life. Everyone assured him that it was just a prop, while Brooks—now inspired by the lunacy—instructed Wilder to treat Feldman like a dog and command him to "get down" and to "drop" the boa.

Once the scene was finally completed to everyone's satisfaction, Brooks noted that Feldman had actually bitten off the foot of the fake fox. And he roared with laughter.

Wilder claimed in his autobiography that they never improvised dialogue on the set, only actions. He recalled how the scene with Igor biting her wrap came to be:

> One day we were filming the scene of Madeline Kahn's arrival at the Frankenstein castle. She was wearing a fox stole and a big turban on her head. The scene seemed flat to all of us. After we tried several things, Mel said, "Marty! When Gene says, 'Eyegore, help me with these bags,' you say, 'Soitanly—you take da blonde, I'll take da one in da toiben.'"
>
> We all laughed and started the scene again, on film. I said my line, Marty said his, and then Marty—in one of his impulsive inspirations—took a huge bite out of the fox fur that Madeline was wearing around her neck, but the tail came off

in his mouth. We all had to go on playing the scene while we looked at Marty with the tail in his mouth. Out of such lunacy great comedy is born.

Igor's line, "Walk this way," in which he advises Frederick to follow him with a tiny cane, was another ad-lib, although it isn't clear who came up with it, Brooks or Feldman. According to Wilder, the gag was inspired by the old "talcum powder" joke from vaudeville, in which a heavy-set woman walks into a drugstore and asks for talcum powder. The clerk, who is bow-legged, says, "Walk this way," and the woman replies, "If I could walk that way I wouldn't need talcum powder!" Wilder stated that Brooks came up with the joke, but in his autobiography, Feldman claimed that he came up with the bit spontaneously on the set to crack up his colleagues, with Brooks insisting that it stay in the film. So you pays your money and you takes your choice as to who's telling the truth here.

During the editing of the film, Brooks was tempted to take the "walk this way" line out because he felt it was too corny. But when the scene got a lot of laughs at an early preview, he decided to leave it in. Good thing too, especially for the rock band Aerosmith, whose members saw the film and were inspired to compose their hit song, "Walk This Way."

Wilder came up with the idea for the scene in which the monster sings "Puttin' on the Ritz" during Frederick's public presentation of his creation at the Bucharest Academy of Science. Brooks didn't like the idea at first, feeling that it was "too silly," and he thought that it would detract too much from the atmosphere of the Universal movies they were trying to recreate. Wilder later said he was "close to rage and tears" about the disagreement and argued passionately to include the scene.

Finally, Brooks relented and said, "It's in!" Wilder, surprised at this sudden turnaround, asked him why he had changed his mind. Brooks told Wilder that since he had fought so forcefully for it, then the only thing to do would be to give it a try. As it turned out, the musical number was one of the high points of the film.

The scene was originally longer, however, and after the monster leaps into the audience, the original cut had included a sequence in which Igor helps the unconscious Frederick back to his feet onstage. In this sequence, Igor has no hump and wears a white tie and tails. When Frederick asks him what happened to his hump, Igor shrugs and says, "Never with tails."

Igor wears some rather unusual footwear during this deleted scene. As he tends to Frederick, he appears to be wearing women's off-white pumps, minus the stiletto heels. Black, fluffy balls of yarn atop his feet complete the eccentric ensemble.

Another song featured in the film, is, strangely enough, "The Battle Hymn of the Republic." Elizabeth sings the patriotic tune while she's brushing her hair. According to Brooks, the song was chosen because (1) it was deliberately incongruous and (2) it was in the public domain. Kahn was actually a gifted singer, and, unlike her character of Lili Von Shtüpp in *Blazing Saddles*, Elizabeth manages to sing on key.

Although all of these stories make the production sound anarchic, Brooks and company had a very clear idea of what they were doing. They had three weeks of rehearsal before filming commenced, as Brooks felt it was essential for the cast to get to know one another. And he gave them specific instructions: They were making a riotous comedy, but their characters didn't know it. At times it should be touching, at times spooky. And it had to be real, with no overacting. On the contrary, the characters shouldn't know that it was funny. The actors were told to do their job and to let the audience decide what was funny.

Brooks's comic philosophy was that there had to be peaks and valleys. "Without information, there is no joke," he wrote in his memoirs. He chose actors who respected the script but who also knew how, and when, to improvise. He felt that, with this cast, he had the best of both worlds. During the three weeks of rehearsal, he felt that they had something special, that the actors worked beautifully together.

After the first few days of shooting, Brooks felt there was something missing in the cinematography when he saw the dailies, but he couldn't quite put his finger on what it was. He asked Hirschfeld what he thought, and the cinematographer seemed quite pleased. Brooks wasn't entirely on board, however, as he felt the look of the film should satirize the Universal movies, and this didn't quite capture that. It was Wilder who came to the defense of Hirschfeld, pointing out to Brooks that they had never told him exactly what they wanted: they had asked him to watch the original *Frankenstein* and *Bride of Frankenstein*, which he had, but they had failed to point out that they wanted something *more*. They wanted to lovingly parody that look. Hirschfeld altered his approach accordingly, and the next few dailies were more on the order of what Brooks wanted.

In *American Cinematographer*, Hirschfeld wrote, "I viewed dusted-off prints of *Frankenstein* and *Bride of Frankenstein*, not to copy, but to satirize. . . . I was about to learn a new type of photography which had nothing to do with mood, or with composition, or with lighting, or sets. It had to do with photographing a 'joke.' The 'joke' was the whole purpose of setting up a scene, and if that didn't come across there was no payoff."

As an example of what he was looking for, Brooks noted later that he and Hirschfeld had only one disagreement during the shoot, and it had to do with a slow track into Wilder's face in one of the laboratory scenes. After a take, Hirschfeld said that he had to do it over again, because there was a noticeable shake in the camera during the tracking shot. Brooks informed him that the shake was what he wanted. Hirschfeld, taken aback, looked at Brooks like he had lost his mind. Brooks went on to explain that what he wanted was "cinematic verisimilitude," the mimicking of the photography in the original *Frankenstein*. In the early 1930s, James Whale wasn't working with the technology of the 1970s; he didn't have a camera mounted on huge rubber wheels gliding along a plywood floor. He did his slow-moving tracks across "a slightly bumpy studio floor," Brooks told Hirschfeld, "and a lot of them had that exact little shake in them." Hirschfeld immediately understood and told Brooks, if that's what he wanted, he'd give it all the shake he would ever need!

Hirschfeld later wrote, "In creating a style for *Young Frankenstein*, I decided that my satire on the 1931 look would be based on over-emphasizing the backlights that were the style in those days, and to really do a black-and-white film that is, keep the middle tones to a minimum; in other words, high contrast. I was able to draw upon past experience from the last black-and-white film that I photographed, *The Incident* (1967)."

Hirschfeld said that it was mostly an issue of lighting. He knew that *Young Frankenstein* should have a specific type of atmosphere and he wanted it to be somewhat realistic, or at least not phony. As the wall of the set was thirty-five feet tall, one of the first things Hirschfeld did during preproduction was to have them painted differently; he felt they were much too dark and that there would most likely be a problem lighting them, so he spoke to Hennesy and asked him to paint the set lighter so that he could control the scenes with his lighting, and Hennesy made haste in giving Hirschfeld what he wanted.

Hirschfeld said that he had a "crackerjack" crew, but he had to watch his camera operator, Tim Vanik, because he had a tendency to laugh quietly to himself when something funny was happening on the set—which it usually was. Hirschfeld could see the camera shaking with Vanik's laughter, and he had to warn him more than once that if he kept laughing and shaking the camera, he would be replaced with someone else. "Somehow the guy got himself under control," Hirschfeld said.

In a later interview, Hirschfeld said,

> My really personal feeling about Mel is that he is a consummate comedic director. I haven't worked with anybody who has his talent. Once I can detach myself from watching my lighting on a take, I'm watching the performance. And I'd say a performance—let's say the monster with Dr. Frankenstein—I'd say that's awfully good and Mel would say, "Let's do it again." It looked perfect to me, but the next take was even better. I don't know what he would say to the actors when he walked up to them, but it was his expertise; sometimes this would go on for three or four takes and each one got better and better.

The laughter on the set was so ubiquitous—and was causing so many takes—that Brooks decided he needed to do something about it. One day, he went out and bought a hundred white handkerchiefs, handed them out to the crew and said to them that if any of them felt like laughing, they could stuff handkerchiefs into their mouths. Brooks claimed that he turned around once during the shooting of a scene and saw a white sea of handkerchiefs in everybody's mouth. He decided then and there that his movie was going to be a hilarious blockbuster.

Brooks said there was one scene in which he could have used a handkerchief himself, but he had given them all out to the crew, so he was helpless. It was the scene in which Frederick, Inga, and Igor are sitting around a table as Frederick bemoans his failure at bringing his creation back to life. Inga, concerned, says to Frederick, "You haven't even touched your food."

Frederick sticks his fingers into his beef stew and boiled potatoes and says sarcastically, "There, now I've touched it. Happy?"

Eager to break this awkward silence, Igor chimes in: "You know, I'll never forget my old dad. When these things would happen to him . . . the things he'd say to me."

Frederick and Inga patiently wait for what Igor is going to say next. "What did he say?" Frederick asks him.

Igor shoots back: "What the hell are you doing in the bathroom day and night? Why don't you get out of there and give someone else a chance!" Then he calmly goes back to eating his boiled potatoes.

Brooks said that he somehow held it together during this take, but the moment the camera stopped rolling, they all "collapsed on the floor and exploded into nonstop laughter." Where's a handkerchief when you need one?

Hirschfeld noted that the interesting thing for him and his crew was learning how to photograph a joke. They wanted the atmospheric, James Whale–styled lighting, but they didn't want to lose the actors' faces, which would have killed the jokes. They used various light sources such as firelight, lightning strikes, and candlelight, not only to heighten the atmosphere but to make sure that the jokes always came through. The audio department also had a lot to deal with, such as the lab equipment that crackled and buzzed.

There were scenes that were technically tricky for the actors. For example, the candles they hold while exploring the castle at night were actually dummy candles made of aluminum pipe with 100-watt projection bulbs inside of them. There was a hollowed-out top into which part of a real candle was placed and lighted; just below within an open slot was a 100-watt projection bulb. A wire ran up each actor's sleeve and down the pantlegs to a dimmer control that had to be kept out of view of the camera. So, in addition to remembering their lines, they had to be careful to properly conceal the wires. The actor's job, in addition to acting, was to keep the open slot of the enclosed bulb from being seen by the camera. This task was tricky when it came to lighting the actors' faces; as the actor passed by the camera, the candle had to be rotated so that the walls would be illuminated. The trick candles were quite touchy and scenes involving them sometimes had to be filmed with extra takes.

The automatic dart-thrower devised by Henry Millar Jr. worked perfectly on the first take, according to Hirschfeld. It was a blow-pipe arrangement that was fired electromagnetically for the sequence in which Frederick throws five bulls-eyes as he attempts to impress Inspector Kemp.

For the scene in which Frederick and Inga explore the secret passageway, the skulls that they find in the anteroom of the laboratory were sculpted by Tuttle out of plaster, fiberglass, wax, false teeth, and monkey hair, all represented in various stages of decay. The skulls are marked "One Year Dead," "Six Months Dead," "Two Months Dead," and "Freshly Dead." That last was not sculpted, but was actually Feldman's head, and after the shock of finding him there, he goes immediately into a brief rendition of, "I Ain't Got Nobody."

There were brains on the set too—not real ones, but sculpted ones. The brain that Igor is sent to steal from the brain depository ("Slip brains under door," the sign reads) is labeled as belonging to "Hans Delbruck, Scientist and Saint." In actual fact, there was a real Hans Delbruck in the nineteenth century; he was a German military historian and a professor at the University of Berlin. He was known for linking warfare to economics and political movements. His son Max, perhaps more to the point, was a twentieth-century biochemist and Nobel laureate. And, just for the record, the notes written on the jars containing the brains in this sequence were written by Brooks himself.

And if we're playing the name game, there was an actual descendant of the real-life House of Frankenstein on the set. British-born Clement von Franckenstein, who was descended from an Austrian family, plays a villager in the film. Originally planning on becoming an opera singer, he didn't quite make the grade so turned to acting instead. Just before appearing in *Young Frankenstein*, he had had an uncredited role in the TV miniseries *QB VII* (1974) as a party guest, and he went on to become a fairly familiar face in television, appearing in episodes of such series as *Falcon Crest*, (1986–1988), *L. A. Law* (1991), and *Murder, She Wrote* (1992). He passed away of hypoxia in 2019 at the age of seventy-four.

Von Franckenstein had originally called himself Clement St. George as he felt "his real name might scare people." He eventually came to embrace his heritage, however, and he was undoubtedly cast in *Young Frankenstein* just because of his name. It would have appealed to Brooks's sense of humor. Ironically, Von Franckenstein only appeared in a few horror films during his acting career, including *Transylvania Twist* (1989) and *The Haunting of Morella* (1990), both for the same director, Jim Wynorski.

There's some debate on where Mary Shelley came across the name "Frankenstein." Some say that she visited Burg Frankenstein (a.k.a. Castle Frankenstein) when she was traveling through Europe with her husband, Percy Shelley. Others say that she never even saw the castle during her journeys down the Rhine, but one thing is for certain: the name "Frankenstein" (or Franckenstein) is a fairly common Germanic name. It arises from "Frank," which is the name of a Germanic tribe, and "stein," which means stone. It literally translates in English as "Stone of the Franks." In any case, having a real "Frankenstein" in *Young Frankenstein* is a stellar in-joke.

One afternoon during filming, Brooks's wife, Anne Bancroft, visited the set. She walked over to Teri Garr during a break in shooting and mentioned to her that she and Mel had just watched *The Conversation* the night before. Garr said to her, "Yeah, that turned out to be a pretty good movie." Bancroft smiled and said, "Honey, *this* is a movie. *The Conversation* is a *film*." Bancroft knew wherof she spoke; after all, she had seduced Dustin Hoffman in a *film* called *The Graduate* (1967).

The climax of Strickfaden's electric "circus" occurred when the monster's body and Frederick were raised from below and the operating platform halted directly beneath the terminal of a gigantic electrode. When Brooks called "Action," Wilder lifted his hands to the heavens, calling upon the power of lightning to give his creation life. With that cue, the special effects team threw switches and an electrical arc whizzed through the air about two feet away from the actor. It jumped from the electrode to the monster's body, with—according to Hirschfeld—about five hundred thousand volts buzzing through the air. Wilder was safe as long as the distance from his body to the electrode was greater than that from the monster's body to the electrode. There was nothing to worry about as far as Boyle was concerned; he wasn't even there, the monster's body being "played" by a dummy. The monster began to smolder, as one does when jarred by half a million volts, and the effect was achieved by hiding smoke machines under the operating table and releasing the smoke slowly through the dummy.

One very old-fashioned technique used on *Young Frankenstein* was the classic process shot, a method of projecting a moving background on a screen behind the performers. This was used in the sequences on the train, in which Brooks chose a night-travel shot to be projected through the train windows. He couldn't locate any stock shots of twisted, gnarled Transylvanian trees for the required eerie landscape, so he was forced to supply his own.

For the sequences in which the villagers were trying to hunt down the monster, Hennesy had designed and built an elaborate forest set that was roughly forty feet deep and one hundred feet long. To get the process shot needed for the background through the train windows, a dolly track was constructed to run parallel to the forest set, and the camera was pushed quickly along the track, standing in, as it were, for the train.

In order to create the illusion of a speeding train, the camera was run at eight frames per second rather than the usual twenty-four, with the dolly grip running as fast as he could. This method ultimately created a thirty-miles-per-hour process plate, which ran only eight seconds on-screen when projected at the usual twenty-four frames per second. This technical problem was solved by placing a large tree trunk at the beginning of the track and another at the end of the track, close to the lens. All editor John C. Howard had to do was to cut exactly when the frame was filled by the tree trunk at the end of the run and spliced onto another print of the exact same scene using the tree trunk at the start of the run. By making a loop of the negative, two hundred feet worth of Transylvanian countryside was seen through the train windows, with the train running thirty miles per hour and lasting for more than two minutes on the process screen; pure movie magic.

There is a shot during the scene involving the lightning storm when the monster's head seems to glow. This effect was accomplished by the special effects crew that included William Tuttle, Henry Millar Jr., Hal Millar, Gary L. King, Jay King, and Robert W. King, who fashioned a mold of Peter Boyle's head, placing a light bulb inside of it and adjusting the brightness with a rheostat. Their jerry-rigging worked very well indeed.

According to Tuttle, it was his own idea to show "something happening with timed electric shocks." He came up with the idea of showing an X-ray of the monster's bones. Hirschfeld later said that Tuttle made a fiberglass cast of Boyle's face and shoulders, fashioning a realistic dummy. Within the fiberglass the special effects aces enclosed some "secret ingredients," items that resembled brains, a skull, and teeth, and when the lights within the skull were pulsed by working a dimmer control up and down, the "creation of life" effect was complete.

Millar Jr., his father Hal, and Jack Monroe "gave life to the night," as Hirschfeld called it, with their low-hanging fog created by a ton and a half of dry ice. They were the ones responsible for the moody opening shot of the film in which the camera prowls around through the courtyard of the castle and the archways within, all while rain pours down and lightning flashes.

As the castle had, in the context of the film, no electricity (except for the laboratory, which was all abuzz), the rooms were lighted by oversized fireplaces, candelabras, and wall sconces. The torches and fireplaces were piped for propane gas and plastered up to look like two-foot-thick stonework. The wall torches had flame spreaders, which added the correct amount of smoke for realism. Concrete logs were used in the fireplaces, as real logs would have presented a fire hazard.

To create the flickering firelight effect, Hirschfeld used silk strips of fabric fluttering in front of two or more lamps placed out of camera range. When the lamps were alternately brightened and darkened with dimmer control, the firelight effect bounced off the walls and the actors with considerable realism.

There was a rumor circulating for many years that the scene in which Frederick accidentally stabs himself with a scalpel while he's speaking to the medical students wasn't in the script, and that Wilder actually stabbed himself in the leg by accident. This rumor is patently false; in fact, sharp-eyed viewers (no pun intended) can spot the square patch under Wilder's pant leg where the scalpel was intended to stab. Method acting only goes so far, after all.

Wilder's propensity for cracking up came to the forefront during the filming of this scene. After Frederick stabbed himself in the thigh, Brooks had to call "Cut!" to avoid seeing the actor break up. In the finished film, he cuts to a close-up of Wilder announcing, "Class dismissed!"

Liam Dunn, who had played Reverend Johnson in *Blazing Saddles*, was cast as Mr. Hilltop, the old man who gets kicked in the groin during Frederick's lecture to the medical students. Dunn had emphysema at the time and the crew always asked him if he needed oxygen or orange juice after every take. Instead, Dunn would always ask for a cigarette, which explains why he had emphysema and why he died of it only two years later.

Other potentially hazardous situations included the scene with Hackman's blind hermit, in which the monster has hot soup spilled on him and his thumb accidentally set on fire. Peter Boyle was well protected, however; he had a pad on his lap to protect him from the soup and a fake thumb covered with alcohol so the fire would continue to burn through several takes.

Sixteen takes were filmed of the monster choking Frederick, which leads to Frederick choking Igor. Brooks and Hirschfeld originally shot them as master cuts, but later had to shoot close-ups in order to cut the sequence together.

Although Brooks kept his word to Wilder about not casting himself in the film, sharp-eyed viewers may note that, when Kemp leaves the castle after the dart game with Frederick, there's a gargoyle on the outer wall of Castle Frankenstein that looks either like Alfred Hitchcock or Mel Brooks, depending on how you look at it. One thing is undeniable, though: when we hear the voice-over of the original Dr. Frankenstein, that voice belongs to Brooks.

Wilder was given a lot of leeway in his performance. He chose to wear the lab coat for most of the movie, and for his street clothes he picked out an old-fashioned English-styled jacket with a belt in the back. "He knew Freddie Frankenstein's style," Brooks quipped. He also wanted to wear a Ronald Colman–type mustache, which Brooks originally vetoed. Wilder was insistent and Brooks finally agreed to shoot two scenes, one with the mustache and one without. Brooks decided that Wilder was right, and that the mustache added *gravitas* to the character. As Brooks later wrote, "Gene was never more handsome than when he played young Dr. Frankenstein. He was also never more insane. The funny-looking Gene Wilder that I had originally met suddenly became a true leading man, albeit slightly crazy."

Brooks felt that Wilder completely understood his character—which he should have, considering the movie was all his idea. He felt that Wilder was intuitive when it came to his performance, and Brooks claimed that he never had to give him "emotional" directions; Wilder knew Frederick's emotions from the get-go. As Brooks wrote, "There was madness in his eyes and fire in his performance."

Wilder said during the making of the film, "[Mel] gives me the most insane things to do, and I carry them out realistically. My job was to make him more subtle. His job was to make me more broad. I would say, 'I don't want this to be *Blazing Frankenstein*,' and he'd answer, 'I don't want an art film that only fourteen people see.'"

On the final day of shooting—May third, 1974—after everyone but Brooks and Wilder had left, Wilder sat down on the edge of the bed that had been used in the scene with him and Garr. He looked up at Brooks and said, "Mel, I've got some more ideas for other scenes from the movie." Brooks said bluntly, "Gene, it's over. We shot it out. It's got a beginning, a middle, and an end. Perfect!"

Wilder, with tears in his eyes, said to Brooks, "Mel, I don't want to go home. I want to stay here. This is the happiest time in my life."

Wilder put it even more succinctly in his memoirs:

On the last day of filming, during our lunch hour, I was sitting in the Frankenstein bedroom set, staring at the fake fireplace. Mel walked in and saw me. "What's the matter? Why so sad?" he asked. "I don't want to leave Transylvania."

Brooks later said that there was "a certain indefinable chemistry" on the set of *Young Frankenstein* that he had never seen before and has never seen since. He called it "kismet," which included the fact that Boyle met his future wife there when she came to visit the set to write an article about the movie. Brooks felt that he had the best of both worlds on this film: he was working with actors who respected the script yet who weren't afraid to improvise.

In the interview with his future wife, Loraine Alterman, for *Rolling Stone* Magazine, Boyle said, "Mel pays a lot of attention to the performers—especially because in a comedy it's the timing. . . . It's got to be right, or it's not funny. . . . Mel's a very hard worker. He has this image of being a lovable nut, but he's an incredibly hard worker."

During the same interview, Alterman asked Feldman about his Igor costume. As he was wont to do, he made a joke about his hump, which turned out to be the type of wardrobe cushion used to make actresses look pregnant. With a straight face (or as straight as Feldman's face could be), he told her, "I have incredible fantasies about it. . . . Was Louis Pasteur in there, or maybe Rosemary's Baby?"

Alterman was also there for the filming of the "love scene" between the monster and Elizabeth in the cave. She described the cave as being approximately ten feet by ten feet, so it was a bit crowded, with the camera on one side aimed at a bed of leaves where Boyle and Kahn would, shall we say, get together. Brooks told the actors that they were only filming above their waists because he was aiming for a PG rating. He also told Boyle that he should start to unzip his fly, which slightly bemused the actor.

When it was time for the actual rehearsal, the cave was crammed not only with lights and camera but with camera assistant, cinematographer, wardrobe person, gaffer, Brooks, Boyle, and Kahn. Alterman wrote of the camera being focused on Kahn, who was lying on the bed of leaves and pine needles, reacting to the monster pulling out his monster-sized organ. Boyle was out of camera range, but miming the motions so Kahn would have something to react to. When she saw it, she started singing, "Ah! Sweet Mystery of life, at last I've found you," and Alterman noted that Brooks was "slightly bent forward clutching his stomach with his left hand and his right hand is extended out like Al Jolson as he mimes the words of the song."

The fact was, when principal photography was completed, it was emotional for everyone in the cast and crew. It may have had to do with the fact that, unlike *Blazing Saddles*, there was a sweetness to *Young Frankenstein* that was something new for Brooks. As he put it, it was his "first attempt at fifty-fifty, laughs and story." It was part love story, part horror parody, and all comedy, but there was an emotional element to it as well. Brooks was fortunate, because for him, *Young Frankenstein* wasn't over at all. In fact, it was just beginning.

Brooks had met John Howard when he had hired him as editor on *Blazing Saddles*. Known professionally as John C. Howard, he had so impressed Brooks on the previous film that he couldn't wait to work with him again. There was good reason for this; Howard was no amateur, having started out as an uncredited assistant editor on Stanley Donen's *Kiss Them for Me* in 1957, a romantic comedy starring Cary

Grant and Jayne Mansfield. By 1969, he had worked his way up to edit-ing George Roy Hill's *Butch Cassidy and the Sundance Kid* and had gone on to edit *A Separate Peace* (1972), four episodes of the hit TV series *The Waltons*, and several other feature and TV projects.

Brooks and Howard had an excellent working relationship. Gener-ally, most editors provide the director with their own rough cut of the film, with the director and the editor collaborating on the final cut. Howard had been nominated for an Oscar for his work on *Blazing Saddles*, on which he and Brooks had collaborated from the get-go. Not wanting to mess with success, Brooks wanted Howard to do the same thing with *Young Frankenstein*, and he didn't want Howard to cut one frame of the film without the director—himself—being there. Brooks wanted each of them to "vote" on every edit, and if Howard didn't agree with Brooks, well, the director overruled him.

In an interview for the DVD, assistant editor Bill Gordon noted, "What begins as a joke doesn't necessarily end up being what's on the screen. You have to baby it and you have to try it many different ways. And it may seem funny to you, but one way, if it's just a character read-ing on camera and it's hysterical, you still have to integrate it with the things that are around it and finding the balance for that."

Gordon also recalled one of the tricks of the trade: "We had a prob-lem in the scene where the operation has been unsuccessful and [Dr. Frankenstein] is very distraught and all of a sudden, they hear the groaning [of the monster] and they run down and they start to let him up; and at that point, there was a lot of dialogue that went on in the scene, and it hadn't been covered in a way so that we could get it out easily. Ultimately, we had to go back to a piece of film that we used in the scene in the bookcase—a piece of Teri Garr—and we blew her up and you'll notice it's a very big head close-up . . . and we put that in so we could sort of jump over a bunch of dialogue that Mel felt was bogging the scene down, and move onto the end of the scene."

Interviewed along with Gordon, Howard said, "What we would do is assemble a reel and he [Brooks] would go around and invite all his secretaries from the lot to come down to the theater and he'd run it. He'd go around a lot and say, 'Can you come to a movie, can you come to a movie?' and they'd see a reel or two and he'd listen to the laughs and rework the work reel."

Gordon noted that Brooks pioneered that approach, which is now common practice. Brooks didn't want studio executives; he wanted people who were as close to "off the street" as he could find on short notice.

Wilder noted that he would see things in the first screening that he didn't think Brooks would want in the final version. Brooks would often tell him that he would keep in those elements for a second screening with, as Wilder put it, "secretaries and butchers and bakers and candlestick makers" to see what the reaction was.

As the writer, Wilder wondered at times what Brooks was doing to his script. Wilder referred to himself as "a director in an embryo state" at this point in his career, and he understood that Brooks was thinking of the whole picture, not any individual scene, but what kind of a movie it was going to be.

Wilder joined Brooks and Howard in the editing room on most occasions. One day, when he saw what Howard had put together, Wilder was not pleased. He later wrote, "When we saw the ascension scene—where I rise with the creature on an elevated platform and cry, 'LIFE, DO YOU HEAR ME? GIVE MY CREATION LIFE!'—my heart sank. I thought this was going to be one of the highlights of the film, and instead it was a boring blob. I put my head down. Mel didn't vomit. Instead, he got up and started banging his head against the wall. He hit it three times, hard."

Then Brooks turned to Wilder and Howard and said, "Let's not get excited! You have just witnessed a fourteen-minute disaster. In one week, you're going to see a twelve-minute fairly rotten scene. In two weeks, you're going to see a ten-minute fairly good scene. And in three weeks, you are going to see an eight-minute masterpiece."

At the time, Wilder felt that that was a fine speech, but he didn't think the scene could be saved. He thought it would have to be reshot.

Wilder later wrote, "The next three weeks were my second lesson in directing: thousands of little pieces of film can be arranged in different ways. Almost three weeks to the day after Mel's speech, the lights went out in the screening room, and I witnessed an eight-minute miracle."

Gordon remembered,

> It so often happens when you're going to your first screening that you want to make sure that everything's playing quickly and there's this panic about . . . is the movie going to be perceived as being slow and dull. Mel was starting to take out some gags and at one point he said, "Well, we're going to take out the gag at the railroad station in Transylvania where Marty says to Gene, 'Walk this way.'" And Stan [assistant editor Stanford C. Allen] says, "No, please, don't do that, please!" And Mel said, "No, it's coming out, it's a cheap joke." And Stan said, "Yeah, it's a cheap joke, but it's funny! Please don't take it out."

So finally, Mel relented and said, "Okay, it'll stay for the preview, but it's coming out Saturday." That scene came on [in the preview] and the audience howled. So we saw Mel on the sidewalk later and said, "So are you taking it out tomorrow?" He said, "Get out of here!" I give Stan the credit for that because Mel may well have taken it out of the movie and you never would have seen it.

By the time they were editing *Young Frankenstein*, *Blazing Saddles* had already been released and had become a huge hit. As a result, Alan Ladd Jr. and 20th Century Fox put all their trust in Brooks and company and let them cut the picture without any interference. By all accounts, the postproduction went smoothly and the first cut they had for a test screening ran two hours and twenty-two minutes long. That may not seem like a very long time compared to today's blockbusters, which routinely run anywhere from two and a half to three hours, but in 1974, that was a pretty long duration, especially for a comedy.

The test screening was set up at the Little Theatre on the Fox studio lot for employees of the studio. Brooks knew that the film ran long; after all, *The Producers* had a running time of only eighty-eight minutes, while *Blazing Saddles* had clocked in at ninety-three minutes. Brooks felt, however, that he didn't want to leave anything out of *Young Frankenstein* that would have clicked with an audience. Perhaps he had had a bit too much fun making the film and had fallen in love with everything they shot; perhaps he was overconfident due to the success of *Blazing Saddles*. Whatever the case, the test screening was not a success; there were laughs, but not as many as Brooks had been hoping for. The film was too long, and the pace dragged.

Brooks realized what the problem was right away, and he addressed the audience after the screening, telling them, "Ladies and gentlemen, you have just seen a two hour and twenty-two-minute failure. In less than three weeks from today, I want you back here to see a ninety-five-minute smash hit movie. I want every one of you back!"

Brooks found that editing could be painful. Like most filmmakers, he was in love with his "baby," but he had to remove the bits that worked against the overall film. His philosophy was that if a scene didn't get a laugh, it should probably be cut. As he wrote later, "Sometimes you have to kill your darlings."

It proved to be more difficult to edit *Young Frankenstein* than it had for *Blazing Saddles*. The previous film had been much more straightforward, going as it did for belly laughs. *Young Frankenstein* was, as Brooks put it, "much more technically eloquent" and Brooks would sometimes find himself stuck between the rock of a beautiful black-and-white shot and the hard place of a hilarious comedy moment. But Brooks didn't want to sacrifice the artistry of the film for the comedy. *Young Frankenstein* was a very different kettle of fish than *Blazing Saddles* had been.

Needless to say, myriad scenes were cut. One of the longest (running at seven minutes and thirty-three seconds) was the scene immediately after the opening credits involving Richard Haydn as Herr Falkstein and fellow film and TV veteran Leon Askin (Billy Wilder's *One, Two, Three*, 1961) as readers of Baron Beaufort von Frankenstein's will to an audience of his relatives. The scene drags on and on with few funny lines until Falkstein plays a recording of the baron's voice that starts to skip and replays the phrase "up yours" several times in a row. Brooks was wise to delete this scene, as it starts the narrative off on the wrong foot and runs much too long.

Another early scene to hit the cutting-room floor also involved Haydn, as he and Frederick are walking down the street. Herr Falkstein is trying to convince Frederick to come to Transylvania to claim his family's estate—which Frederick doesn't want to bother with—when the two men pass a street musician who's playing the Eastern European lullaby that becomes the monster's theme later in the film. Frederick finds the tune "curiously haunting" and stops to ask the violinist what the tune is called. He tells him it's "an old Transylvanian lullaby." Frederick asks if he can see his violin, to which the violinist is agreeable. Frederick takes the violin and breaks it in half over his knee, then hands it back to the puzzled and bemused musician. When Falkstein asks him why he did that, Frederick denies ever doing it and asks him if he's insane. "He *is* a Frankenstein!" Falkstein declares, seemingly to the heavens, and Frederick finally agrees to travel to Transylvania to collect his inheritance.

This scene makes very little sense, as we have not yet heard the lullaby or ascertained its importance in the film. Frederick's reaction to the music doesn't make sense either, and it's easy to see why this scene was scrapped: in addition to being pointless, it isn't funny.

A short scene in which Inspector Kemp comes to the door of the Frankenstein castle, which is answered by a seductive Inga in a slinky gown, was also cut. He asks to see Frederick, and at least this scene reveals why Kemp has a wooden arm. Frederick asks him if it was a war injury, and he tells him that it was in fact the Frankenstein monster who tore his arm off—just as in *Son of Frankenstein*. Mars completely dominates this brief sequence, and it does give us a bit more insight into his character. Ultimately, though, Brooks decided that the scene was not needed.

Another short sequence—in which the monster, loose in the village, encounters a robber—goes nowhere. A scene in which Frederick and Inga get into a clinch, with Wilder desperately trying to resist her charms so he won't be unfaithful to his fiancée, could have easily stayed in the movie, however. Wilder's comedic timing here is as impeccable as anywhere in the film, and his attempts to recall the speed of light in a romantic context is quite funny. As for Garr, she's never been more smolderingly sexy—and at the same time, charmingly comedic—than in this brief interlude.

One more deleted scene of note involves the monster's Bar Mitzvah, in which he is referred to as "Young Franklin Stein." Brooks essentially cut his movie in half, taking out the jokes that didn't work or any sequences that slowed down the pace of the film.

Brooks wound up going back to the days of James Whale for the transitions—wipes, iris shots, and spins. He felt that the results of this technique were twofold: it helped to establish the feeling of a thirties Whale film, and they also eased the transition from the artistry and the comedy.

Brooks worked day and night to get his "darling" into the proper shape. Keeping in the spirit of James Whale, he went back to thirties-style editing techniques. Occasionally, rather than eliminating a scene completely, he and Howard simply cut it down to something more manageable or rearranged it. As Brooks wrote, "There is a lot you can change without reshooting. Hundreds of little pieces of film can be arranged in hundreds of different ways."

He had promised his screening audience that he would return with his "rearranged" film in three weeks; it was more than three weeks later—nearly three months later, in fact—when he gathered most of the same audience at the Little Theater for another screening. It wasn't until then that Brooks had a cut of the film that he felt was good enough. As Brooks later wrote, "It went like gangbusters! The audience not only laughed their heads off, but there was a palpable feeling of sweet sadness when the film ended."

Young Frankenstein was the fourth collaboration between Brooks and his favorite composer, John Morris. After scoring *The Producers*, *The Twelve Chairs*, and *Blazing Saddles*, Brooks and Morris had a kind of shorthand between them, and when Brooks asked him to compose a melody that would define the emotion of *Young Frankenstein*, Morris came up with "Transylvanian Lullaby," a theme that echoed those of composers Frank Skinner and Hans J. Salter for the old Universal horror films. Brooks felt that the theme captured the soul of the monster, and when Morris conducted the orchestra in the recording session for the opening title music, first violinist Jerry Vinci played an obbligato (a countermelody) that Brooks said brought tears to his eyes.

The studio felt that December 1974 would be a good time to release the film, striking while the iron was still hot from *Blazing Saddles*. December 15 was the date chosen, and Brooks's comedy would be competing at the box office with *The Towering Inferno*, which would open on the 14th, and Francis Ford Coppola's *The Godfather Part II*, which would open on the 20th. That kind of competition was enough to give any filmmaker pause, even one who was riding high on the success of *Blazing Saddles*.

As it turned out, Brooks had nothing to worry about. He and his cast and crew had created a monster, and it was now loose in the countryside.

11

"ABBY NORMAL"

Young Frankenstein opened at the Sutton Theater in New York. Wilder and some of the other principals flew in from Los Angeles for the premiere. It was a midnight screening on a Thursday so the movie could qualify for the weekend grosses. All those involved in the movie were very nervous about how it would be received. The lights dimmed, the titles came on—and the audience applauded. The poster, designed by Anthony Goldschmidt and John Alvin, who had performed the same duties on *Blazing Saddles*, had given the audience some idea of what to expect; it featured Wilder with his most crazed "Dr. Frankenstein" expression along with Peter Boyle as the monster in a top hat.

At that time, Goldschmidt was one of the top graphic designers in Hollywood, while Alvin, a fine artist in his own right, had formed his own company after the success of *Blazing Saddles*. There were several conceptual designs for *Young Frankenstein* before the two created the one we know and love; at one point, the poster depicted the monster and Frederick wearing their tuxedoes in their dancing pose, but underneath them is the hand-painted title, dripping blood. That was under consideration for the final poster, but it was ultimately rejected because it was felt that the blood didn't really represent the mood or scope of the film.

According to Goldschmidt, who was later quoted in the book *The Art of John Alvin*, the artist was young and quite serious about his work, and at times he would be frustrated after meeting with Brooks, who tended to be "Mel Brooks the comedian" if there were more than three people in the room. At one particular meeting, Alvin presented concept sketches and Brooks kept asking for everything to be "bigger." Alvin's retort was that if everything was bigger, then nothing would look big. Brooks was adamant, however. Alvin, somewhat exasperated, finally handed Brooks his pencil and said, "Show me." Brooks cracked up, which ended the stand-off.

Ultimately, Brooks got his wish: the poster was painted on the billboard of the Playboy Building on Sunset Strip, resulting in its fame as being the biggest billboard up to that time. The billboard was some 5,600 square feet, requiring 86,000 gallons of paint and fourteen klieg lights to make sure everyone saw it. As Michael Gruskoff said, "It was unmissable."

Brooks contacted Hugh Hefner, and they screened the film at the Playboy Mansion. As it happened, Hefner loved classic horror movies and he had even made an amateur Frankenstein film when he was a teenager. He fell head over heels in love with *Young Frankenstein* and showed it again to his friends the following evening.

According to Goldschmidt, Alvin painted the final poster in oil on canvas at forty by sixty inches. The major change was in the look of Wilder's face: the studio insisted on a shot taken from the film, so Alvin was required to paint over the old face and replace it with the new one.

According to Gruskoff, he and the other producers were laughing so hard viewing the dailies that they were hoping it would all work out as well as it seemed during production. He rode with Brooks and his wife, Anne Bancroft, to the sneak preview in San Bernadino. After they saw the audience reaction, all their fears were allayed and they were ecstatic.

There was a so-called people's premiere at the Avco Theater in Westwood, Los Angeles; and there were lines around the block, which pleased Brooks to no end. It turned out that the studio's fears regarding the film being in black and white were not only unfounded, but the reverse turned out to be true: people went to see it in part *because* it was in black and white. That made it different, and in the seventies, different was good.

Also, because *Blazing Saddles* had been such a box-office sensation, audiences flocked to *Young Frankenstein* to see what Brooks would do next. In 107 weeks of release around the world, the film grossed $86,273,333, an extraordinary amount of money for that time, especially for a film with a budget of $2.8 million. In today's numbers, its box-office gross would amount to $413 million adjusting for inflation. Alan Ladd Jr. was especially pleased, as the film's success enabled him to greenlight over three hundred films during his career, including *Star Wars*, *Alien*, *A Fish Called Wanda*, *Thelma and Louise*, *Blade Runner*, and many more now-legendary productions.

Ladd noted later that he "just went along for the ride" on *Young Frankenstein*. As he pointed out, the early seventies were a time when Hollywood allowed filmmakers to make more personal movies than they do today, when nearly everything that gets greenlit seems to be a part of a franchise. As he put it, "Now it's very corporate. . . . The studios don't have their own personalities now. It's very different."

As Gruskoff recalled in the DVD interview, "We opened it up around Christmas time in '74 and there were a lot of very big movies, and so the competition was going to be really, really tough. And there we were, you know, doing business like *Blazing Saddles*, which was also a big hit. So, because of those two films, Mel became a major player in town, and prior to *Blazing Saddles*, he couldn't get arrested for three years."

And most critics loved Brooks's latest hit as much as audiences, some even more so because they knew exactly what he was parodying. In his review headlined "*Young Frankenstein* a Monster Riot," Vincent Canby of the *New York Times* raved,

> Mel Brooks's funniest, most cohesive comedy to date. . . . Although it hasn't as many roof-raising boffs as *Blazing Saddles*, it's funnier over the long run because it is more disciplined. The anarchy is controlled. Mel Brooks sticks to the subject, recalling the clichés of horror films of the 1930s as lovingly as someone remembering the small sins of youth. . . . Perhaps the nicest thing about *Young Frankenstein* is that one can laugh with it and never feel as if the target film, James Whale's 1931 classic that starred Boris Karloff, is being rudely used.

Chicago Sun-Times critic Roger Ebert enthused,

> *Young Frankenstein* is as funny as we expect a Mel Brooks movie to be, but it's more than that: It shows artistic growth and a more sure-handed control of the material by a director

who once seemed willing to do literally anything for a laugh. It's more confident and less breathless. . . . From its opening title (which manages to satirize *Frankenstein* and *Citizen Kane* at the same time) to its closing, uh, refrain, *Young Frankenstein* is not only a Mel Brooks movie but also a loving commentary on our own love-hate affairs with monsters. This time, the monster even gets to have a little love-hate affair of his own.

In the *Los Angeles Times*, Charles Champlin called *Young Frankenstein* "a likable, unpredictable blending of slapstick and sentiment," while the anonymous critic in *Variety* noted, "The screen needs one outrageously funny comedy each year, and *Young Frankenstein* is an excellent follow-up for the enormous audiences that howled for much of 1974 at *Blazing Saddles*," failing to point out that *Young Frankenstein* was also a 1974 release, although most of its playdates were in 1975.

Of course, there had to be some naysayers. Ebert's compatriot at the *Chicago Tribune*, Gene Siskel, only gave the movie three stars, writing, "Part homage and part send-up, *Young Frankenstein* is very funny in its best moments, but they're all too infrequent." In the *Washington Post*, Gary Arnold—who also disliked *Blazing Saddles*, so what was wrong with this guy?—complained, "Wilder and Brooks haven't dreamed up a funny plot. They simply rely on the old movie plots to get them through a rambling collection of scene parodies." Talk about missing the point! Then again, Tom Milne of the rather snooty *Monthly Film Bulletin* in the UK carped, "All too often Brooks resorts to the most cliched sort of *Carry On* smut," referring to that long and quite beloved British series of films that relied heavily on double-entendres and boob jokes.

But these party poopers had absolutely no effect on the popularity of *Young Frankenstein*, and they were not wise in their generation: the movie went on to become one of Brooks's most beloved films and another cultural touchstone. Its place in cinema history is assured to this day and beyond.

In my interview with him, Steve Haberman told me,

> Gene Wilder's comedies after Mel Brooks are not good. That's because, even though Wilder came up with the idea for *Young Frankenstein*, and he wrote the script with Mel, it's Mel's vision. He let Gene talk him into "Puttin' on the Ritz" and didn't regret it, because it's a huge part of the movie and it's a funny, funny bit. It was a clever bit, but Mel made it a clever and warm bit. Mel made it the love story of two men. One created the other. He gave it that, and he did the same thing with Frankenstein and Igor. One had nothing in common with the other, but there's a love affair, a bond, like Bialystock and Bloom. It's like Frank Langella and Ron Moody in *The Twelve Chairs*.
>
> Mel is like Howard Hawks; Hawks could do a movie in every genre—science fiction, westerns, detective stories, musicals, whatever—and it turned into a Howard Hawks movie because he had a very distinctive vision. His movies are about self-respect and professionalism, about bonding with people you need to get the job done. Whether it's a western or a war movie, that's what every Howard Hawks movie is about. That's what *Gentlemen Prefer Blondes* is about, except the two guys

are two girls, but they respect each other because they're good at gold digging. That's their job.

And Mel is that way too. Mel is so cute, because he let me make this documentary about him, which is on a boxed set of Blu-rays called *The Incredible Mel Brooks*. It's Blu-rays that have non-feature stuff, and one of those Blu-rays is a little documentary called *Mel and His Movies*. What I did was, I went through all of Mel's movies chronologically and interviewed Mel, and had access to all the film clips and all the songs, and Mel paid for all that stuff. If you put them all together, it's like a three-hour documentary on Mel as a filmmaker. In the course of doing that, I said, "Mel, you're an *auteur*," and he said, "No, no," and I said, "Yeah, you are!" And I talked to him like I'm talking to you about his themes and his visual style and his style of comedy and the way he sees people. And he's so cute in an interview that's online someplace, he says, "Yeah, Steve Haberman is a canny son of a bitch. He came to me and he said, 'You're an *auteur*,' and he just gave me clues and I finally came up with the idea that my theme is 'love or money.' The characters are always going for love or money.'" And that's true in a way, if money is a metaphor. Like in *Young Frankenstein*, the theme is love or creating life, love or being God. It's always love or something else, and it's generally between two guys.

Haberman said he's a big fan of Brooks's work and recalled meeting Brooks long before he worked with him:

Mel tells this story: When I was at USC, he was screening *Young Frankenstein* at the auditorium there. And I was there, and when he came out of the screening—which was very successful, everybody was patting him on the back—he walked by me. He didn't know me and I said, "That was a great movie, Mr. Brooks." And he said, "Thank you, kid, keep in touch!"

So, years later, when I sold him *Life Stinks* and we made the movie, I told him that story, and he tells that story to everybody. He says, "This kid! He was just a kid at USC and I screened *Young Frankenstein* and I came out and he said, 'That was a great movie,' and I said, 'Thanks, kid, keep in touch,' which I say to everybody. And he's the only one who kept in touch, and look at him now!"

Haberman went on to say that he was only a part of Mel's vision:

"I think that, even though the projects were initiated by me, they went through that mixture, that sausage grinder that came out as Mel Brooks's vision. He had the final word on everything. And they're obviously him. I wouldn't have made a movie like *Life Stinks*. I don't give a crap about homeless people. But Mel did. Even though I came up with the story, in my opinion, it was just a clever story idea that I had. But he brought the form to it, and he brought the love for the people to it. We both came up with the comedy, but *his* comedy was very embracing.

When I pointed out to Haberman that what sets Brooks's parodies apart from other filmmakers' is his love of what he's parodying, Haberman responded, "Yeah, he loves westerns and old classics, and otherwise he wouldn't have made them [parodies]. You know, he sat down with Hitchcock and Hitchcock pitched ideas to Mel for *High Anxiety*. Mel thought he was funnier than Hell."

Brooks, ninety-seven years of age at this writing, doesn't think that *Young Frankenstein* is his funniest movie—he feels that honor should go to *Blazing Saddles*—but he does feel that it's his *best* movie. In a 2013 interview marking the fortieth anniversary of both films for *Parade* magazine by Michele "Wojo" Wojciechowski, Brooks said,

> If you do it for you, the audience really appreciates it because they're so much smarter than people in the business think.
>
> It's still a smart, deeply intelligent, bright movie. The audience gets it, they always appreciate it, and it always works. . . . It works to this day. . . . If I go someplace, somebody will always yell, "*Young Frankenstein* rules!"

And does it still "rule" fifty years after it was produced? To this writer, it certainly does. Everything about it *works* and works beautifully. It's a work of art as much as it is a comedy, and it's a high-water mark of the comedy-horror genre, among many other virtues. Let's try and break it down, piece by piece—stitch by stitch, as it were—into its various parts.

In the title role of the original Dr. Frankenstein's grandson, Wilder is pure comic genius. As Canby wrote in his review, "This Dr. Frankenstein is a marvelous addled mixture of young Tom Edison, Winnie the Pooh and your average *Playboy* reader with a keen appreciation of beautiful bosoms."

Although Wilder is sometimes the straight man to Feldman, he can hold his own with the best of the one-liners, as witness this exchange between Frankenstein and Igor:

> Igor: Dr. Frankenstein . . .
>
> Frankenstein: That's "Fronkensteen."
>
> Igor: You're putting me on.
>
> Frankenstein: No, it's pronounced Fronkensteen.
>
> Igor: Do you also say "Froaderick?"
>
> Frankenstein: No, Frederick.
>
> Igor: Well, why isn't it Froaderick Fronkensteen?
>
> Frankenstein: It isn't. It's Frederick Fronkensteen.
>
> Igor: I see.
>
> Frankenstein: You must be Igor.
>
> Igor: No, it's pronounced "Eye-Gor."
>
> Frankenstein: But they told me it was "Ee-Gor."
>
> Igor: Well, they were wrong then, weren't they?

The scene in which Frankenstein discovers that Igor has brought him an abnormal brain that he has just placed in the head of his creation shows Wilder at his controlled yet crazed peak. Suspecting the worst, Frankenstein asks Igor, "Now that brain you gave me . . . was it Hans Delbruck's?"

"No," Igor answers.

"Ah, very good," Frankenstein says, still trying to be as calm as possible. "Would you mind telling me whose brain I *did* put in?"

Looking sheepish, Igor says, "You won't be angry?"

Trying very hard to retain his composure, Frankenstein assures him, "I will *not* be angry."

"Abby someone," Igor replies.

Frankenstein pauses, then says simply, "Abby someone. Abby who?"

"Abby . . . Normal," Igor responds.

Frankenstein pauses, then repeats, "Abby Normal?"

Igor says, "I'm almost sure that was the name."

Frankenstein chuckles slightly, still trying to remain calm, then says, "Are you saying that I put an abnormal brain into a seven and a half foot long, fifty-four inch wide *gorilla*?"

He grabs Igor and starts throttling him. "Is that what you're telling me?" he shouts, with a demented look in his eyes. In a matter of seconds, Wilder has gone from a surface rationality to the lunacy of a truly mad doctor, and he does this sort of flip-flop throughout the picture. His comic range is absolutely extraordinary.

Another example of that range occurs when Frederick goes into the cell where the monster is chained to a large chair. Before he enters, Frederick turns to Inga and Igor and says, rationally, calmly, and confidently, "Love is the only thing that can save this poor creature, and I am going to convince him that he is loved even at the cost of my own life. No matter what you hear in there, no matter how cruelly I beg you, no matter how terribly I may scream, do not open this door or you will undo everything I have worked for. Do you understand? Do not open this door."

"Yes, doctor," Inga assures him.

"Nice working with ya," says Igor.

Frederick walks into the room, shutting the door behind himself. When the monster wakes up and growls at him, the good doctor changes his tune. As Brooks put it years later, "He goes from this commanding doctor to a scared kid banging on the door and screaming."

"Let me out!" Frederick pleads. "Let me out of here! Get me the hell out of here! What's the matter with you people? I was joking! Don't you know a joke when you hear one? HA, HA, HA, HA! *Jesus Christ, get me out of here! Open this goddamn door or I'll kick your rotten heads in! Mommy!*"

As Brooks wrote, "Talk about range! He went all the way emotionally from A to Z. I loved sitting in a theater, watching that scene, as the audience exploded into gales of laughter all around me."

Finally, Frederick regains his composure and says to the monster, "Hello, handsome! You're a good-looking fellow, do you know that? People laugh at you, people hate you, but why do they hate you? Because . . . they are jealous! Look at that boyish face. Look at that sweet smile. Do you wanna talk about physical strength? Do you want to talk about sheer muscle? Do you want to talk about the Olympian ideal? You are a God! And listen to me; you are not evil. YOU. ARE. GOOD."

The monster starts to cry and Frederick hugs him. "This is a nice boy. This is a good boy," Frederick assures him. "This is a mother's angel. And I want the world to know once and for all, and without any shame, that we love him. I'm going to teach you. I'm going to show you how to walk, how to speak, how to move, how to think. Together, you and I are going to make the single greatest contribution to science since the creation of fire."

From outside, Inga calls, "Dr. Fronkensteen! Are you all right?"

As the music swells on the soundtrack, Frederick answers: "*My name is Frankenstein!*"

The supporting players couldn't have been better. Feldman, who had already appeared on American television on *The Dean Martin Show* and *Marty Feldman's Comedy Machine*, turned out to be the perfect choice for Igor ("It's pronounced Eye-Gore"). With his bug-eyes (actually the result of his thyroid condition, called Grave's Disease) and impeccable comic timing, Feldman is one of the greatest and most consistent delights of the film.

The pop-eyed Feldman's timing never falters. Take, for example, the scene in which Igor and Frederick are exhuming a body and Frederick complains, "What a filthy job!" Igor's response is "It could be worse." Frederick asks, "How?" "Could be raining," says Igor. On cue, it starts to pour. Their po-faced reaction is straight out of Laurel and Hardy.

Feldman sets the tone of his character perfectly in his first meeting with Frederick at the train station. Frederick points out, "You know, I'm a rather brilliant surgeon. Perhaps I could help you with that hump." Igor says simply, "What hump?"

"To me," Wilder said in the DVD interview, "[Marty] is probably the heart and soul of the film. The bizarre world that we all entered into when we walked onto that set was epitomized by Marty Feldman."

Igor's non sequiturs continue throughout the film. When Frederick, Inga, and Igor find an abandoned violin in the depths of the castle, Frederick says, "Well, this explains the music." Igor plucks the violin and reports, "It's still warm."

At one point, exasperated with Igor, Frederick says to him, "Damn your eyes!" Igor smiles, looks at the camera, and says, "Too late."

He gets a lot of mileage out of his hunchback status too. Before they find the violin, he says to Frederick, "I heard the strangest music from the upstairs kitchen and I just . . . followed it down. Call it . . . a hunch." Then he makes the sound of a drum roll: "Ba-dum chi!"

Igor also has a tendency to be a bit lecherous, as when, shortly after Elizabeth arrives, he tells Frederick, "It's gonna be a long night. If you need any help with the girls, I'll be . . . "

It seems incredible at this late date that Tom Milne of *The Monthly Film Bulletin* complained about Feldman's "grotesquely unfunny mugging." All I can say about Milne is that he must have been no fun at parties. Feldman is one of the most consistently hilarious elements of *Young Frankenstein*, so much so that he became an instant member of Brooks's stock company (he next appeared in the director's *Silent Movie*, 1976), and costarred with Wilder in the latter's first directorial effort, *The Adventure of Sherlock Holmes' Smarter Brother* the year after the release of *Young Frankenstein*, and ended up directing and starring in *The Last Remake of Beau Geste* (1977) before his untimely death from a heart attack in 1982 at the age of forty-eight. Feldman remains a fondly remembered comic figure of the seventies, and, if he had never appeared in anything beyond *Young Frankenstein*, he'd still be a comedy icon.

As Elizabeth—one of the few characters actually taken from Shelley's novel—Kahn equals her performance in *Blazing Saddles*, with the additional advantage of having more screen time than in the previous film. Mind you, her version of Elizabeth is a far cry from the one that Shelley conceived; for one thing, she doesn't want Frankenstein to embrace her at the railway station because her taffeta dress "wrinkles so easily." And that's only one of her upscale, high-maintenance idiosyncrasies. When he moves to kiss her, she admonishes him with, "No tongues!"

Her upper-class snootiness is gone with the wind, however, after the monster kidnaps her and takes her to a cave where he has his way with her. Gazing upon his manhood, Elizabeth whimpers: "Woof!" Post-coitus, she breaks into song: "Oh, sweet mystery of life, at last I've found you! At last I know the secret of it all."

At that point, the monster seems distracted and heads for parts unknown. This vexes Elizabeth, who complains, "Oh, where are you going? You men are all alike. Seven or eight quick ones and then you're out with the boys to boast and brag. You better keep your mouth shut! Oh . . . I think I love him!"

Although Kahn isn't quite as raucous in *Young Frankenstein* as she was in *Blazing Saddles*—in part due to the more subdued character— she certainly solidifies her reputation as one of the great comedians of her era. In 1974 she was on a roll, just as her mentor Brooks was, and she lights up the screen whenever she appears as Elizabeth.

The big surprise of *Young Frankenstein* was the spot-on comedic per-formance of Cloris Leachman. Considered a serious actress up to that point, Leachman, who had done notable work in such episodic televi-sion as "It's a Good Life" (1962) on *The Twilight Zone* and "Premoni-tion" (1955) on *Alfred Hitchcock Presents*, among many others, matches everyone stroke for stroke in *Young Frankenstein*. The offscreen horses whinnying every time her name is mentioned is a gag that's consis-tently funny—whether it's because it's German for "glue" or, as Brooks said, he got the name from a German general named Blucher—and her comic delivery is absolutely faultless.

Leachman's sense of the absurd shines through in every scene in which she appears. Brooks had instructed her from the start to portray Frau Blucher as a Teutonic version of Mrs. Danvers from *Rebecca*, complete with a mole on her cheek. The exchange between her and Frederick, which ends with Frederick saying, "Then you and Victor were . . . " and Frau Blucher finishing with, *"Yes! Yes!* Say it . . . He vas my *boyfriend!"* is one of the funniest moments in the film.

Leachman's comic German accent provides laughs just about every time she has any dialogue, even something as seemingly innocuous as, "Stay close to the candles. The stairvay can be . . . treacherous." It's all in the delivery, such as this earlier exchange between Frederick and Blucher:

Blucher: Would the doctor care for . . . a brandy before retiring?

Frederick: No, thank you.

Blucher: (somewhat suggestively) Some varm milk . . . perhaps?

Frederick: No, thank you very much. No thanks.

Blucher: (more suggestively) Ovaltine?

Frederick: *Nothing!* Thank you. I'm a little tired.

Blucher: Then I vill say . . . goodnight, Herr Doctor.

Frederick: Goodnight, Frau Blucher.

And, of course, the horses whinny outside.

Frau Blucher disappears about midway through the film. Although everyone else manages to carry the rest the rest of the show, she is missed.

Teri Garr had come a long way from such movies as *A Swingin' Affair* (1963, her film debut) and appearing uncredited in several Elvis Presley vehicles as a background dancer. Her comedic timing in *Young*

Frankenstein is every bit as good as that of the more seasoned veterans. Who could ever forget the introduction to her character, Inga, when she asks Frankenstein if he wants a roll in the hay? Frankenstein raises one eyebrow and starts to stutter, at which point Inga smiles sweetly and then proceeds to literally roll in the hay, all while singing, "Roll, roll, roll in ze hay!" in her ersatz German accent.

Inga is a charming if rather thick character and Garr makes the most of her screen time. She's also a good sport, as some of the lines involving her are rather sexist, such as when Frederick spies the enormous door knockers on the castle and exclaims, "What knockers!" to which Inga shyly says, "Oh, thank you, doctor."

Then there's the sequence in which Frederick is about to perform the experiment that will give his creation life, during which he has to be elevated on the table with the creature to the roof of the castle. He says to Inga, "Well, dear, are you ready?" "Yes, doctor," she replies. "Elevate me," he commands. "Now? Right here?" Inga says incredulously. "Yes. Yes, raise the platform." "Oh, ze platform!" she responds. "Oh, zat, yah, yah . . . yes."

Boyle's impressive height was one reason he was cast as the monster, but he ultimately turned out to be very funny indeed. One needs only to view his "Puttin' on the Ritz" scene to observe that this excellent dramatic actor is also a gifted comic performer, who later won a couple of Emmy Awards for his performance on the TV series *Everybody Loves Raymond*.

In fact, one of the funniest scenes in *Young Frankenstein* involves two "serious" actors, Boyle and Hackman. Sounds like a law firm, doesn't it? Apparently, Brooks and Wilder saw something in the Oscar-winning actor that nobody else had noticed. The scene with him as the blind hermit attempting to befriend Boyle as the monster is a comic gem from start to finish. Based directly on the similar scene in *Bride of Frankenstein* featuring Karloff and a character actor called O. P. Heggie, it parodies the original perfectly. From the point when Hackman opens the door to discover "an incredibly big mute" to the moment when he inadvertently lights the monster's thumb on fire thinking it's a cigar, this sequence gets some of the biggest belly laughs in the entire film, topped by Hackman standing alone in the doorway and lamenting, "I was gonna make espresso."

As Wilder put it in the DVD interview, "The blind man pours soup into the monster's soup bowl in *Bride of Frankenstein*; I thought, wouldn't it be wonderful if he misses. . . . [T]here was almost an equivalent for each thing that happens. 'Food good.' 'Friend good.' It wasn't that we were doing a burlesque. It wasn't the Three Stooges—except the soup came close to that. But it was still in control and then the cigars and the thumb being lit . . . it was really a parody of that beautiful scene in *Bride of Frankenstein*."

The scene in which the monster is choking the life out of Frederick, who is forced to mime a game of charades, was a difficult one to film because Boyle was concerned that he might accidentally hurt Wilder, who he said kept moving while his arms were around his neck. Supposedly, Brooks quipped, "Look, if Gene dies, he dies!" to which Wilder responded, "Hey, wait a minute!"

The scene also involved Feldman lighting a match; sometimes the match would light, and in other takes, it wouldn't. Sometimes it would light, but the flame would sputter, and it wasn't enough to "frighten" the monster. Somehow, they got through the scene after numerous takes, and the rest is comedy history.

Another great scene is a parody of the sequence in Whale's original *Frankenstein* in which the monster encounters a little girl by a lake. In Whale's film, the little girl (Marilyn Harris) ends up drowning after being thrown into the lake by the monster. The reason for this tragedy is that the girl, who seems totally innocent and unafraid of the monster, is throwing daisy petals into the water to watch them float "like boats." Sadly, she runs out of daisy petals and the monster throws her into the lake to see if *she* floats. She doesn't.

Brooks's version has a happier (and funnier) ending, which was actually written by Wilder. In imitation of the 1931 film, the monster and the little girl (Anne Beesley, who appeared two years later in the two-part TV movie *Sybil*) run out of things to throw into the water. We see the monster in close-up, apparently thinking to himself that it might be fun to throw the *girl* into the water. Then, however, we cut to a shot of the girl's parents (Michael Fox and Lidia Kristen) wondering where she'd gone off to, and then back to a shot of the monster and the girl, who are now playing on a seesaw. When the monster sits on his end of the seesaw, his weight catapults the girl, who is sitting on the other end, through the air, through her window, and into her own bed, where her parents—who had been concerned about her whereabouts—find her, apparently sleeping peacefully. All is well.

The effect of the little girl flying through the air was achieved by placing the girl on wires, which were painted to conceal them based on the lighting. In twenty-first-century filmmaking, wires can be removed easily in postproduction with the aid of a computer. Obviously, such technology was not available in 1974, so it was done the old-fashioned way—and very effectively too. As Brooks put it, Beesley—who he said was "very bossy"—"flew like a missile." Brooks also assured that no wires would be seen by clever editing in which he used cutaways to the monster's face, picking up on the little girl when she lands on her bed.

As for the sequence that has no counterpart in the original Universal movies—the "Puttin' on the Ritz" song and dance routine—Brooks was wise to go along with Wilder after their little disagreement. It's a standout scene in the movie. The audience I saw *Young Frankenstein* with in 1975 was doubled over in laughter every time Boyle launched into the refrain in his "monster" voice—"Pootin' on a Reetz!"—and it's now considered to be one of the highlights of the movie. Brooks and Wilder, as previously noted, had violently disagreed about including the scene—he claimed they almost got into a fistfight over it—with Wilder believing that it was Frankenstein's proof of how incredible his creation was, and Brooks insisting that it was too silly and would destroy the continuity of the film. They finally came to an agreement whereupon Brooks would film it, and if the test audience reaction was negative, it would be taken out.

Brooks later wrote,

> I filmed it, and after the reaction at our first test screening, I turned to Gene and said, "Gene, you were absolutely right. Not only does it work, but it may be one of the best things about the whole movie."
>
> I have never been so wrong in my life. I think I ate more humble pie on that day than ever before. Gene was right because it took the movie to another level. We left satire and made it our own. It was new, different, crazy and had the audience laughing out of control.

The "Puttin' on the Ritz" scene was filmed at the Mayfair Music Hall in Santa Monica. Built in 1911, the Mayfair was a vaudeville-style theater and a perfect location for the sequence. It was, however, a small venue and difficult to light. Kenneth Mars and the actor who played his assistant, Richard Roth, were placed at the back of the theater, and it was problematic to light them as Brooks didn't want the master shot to be over-lit. Hirschfeld ultimately placed lights in the back so they could film the sequence, which took about five days in total.

Brooks hired Alan Johnson, who had choreographed "Springtime for Hitler," to arrange the sequence. Johnson assisted Brooks in teaching Wilder and Boyle the intricate dance steps, working out the timing not only with the taps, but with the cane that Boyle uses. After all the arguments with Wilder, it was Brooks himself who came up with the idea of the monster singing the extended line, "Puttin' on the Riiiiitz." Brooks told Boyle that he didn't have to worry about staying in key, that the monster would sing enthusiastically, and he advised him to "blow his top." Brooks claimed later that he kept having to yell "Cut!" because the audience of extras kept cracking up, blowing the scene. He reminded them that Boyle was the monster, and they should be afraid of him.

Although Kenneth Mars's accent is so thick he's unintelligible throughout the film—which is part of the joke—the scene in which he plays darts with Wilder is a pitch-perfect parody of a nearly identical scene in Rowland V. Lee's *Son of Frankenstein* in which Lionel Atwill's Inspector Krogh plays darts with a nearly hysterical Basil Rathbone as Wolf Frankenstein. Mars's Inspector Kemp, like Atwill's character, has a wooden arm, which is used to comic effect as a battering ram in a later scene.

It's the attention to detail that makes *Young Frankenstein* soar over most horror parodies. Unlike, say, *Scary Movie* (2000) and its descendants, which derided their source material, Brooks and Wilder love it, and it shows. They've seen the films they're gently mocking hundreds of times and know their every nuance. Ultimately, *Young Frankenstein* is probably most effective when viewed by film buffs, but it's written, directed, and performed in such a way that its wacky, off-kilter, and outright silly humor can be enjoyed by anyone, including Joe Six-Pack, his wife, and their little kids.

Everyone has a favorite line from *Young Frankenstein*, whether it's "What knockers!" or "Say it! He vas my *boyfriend!*" or even when Wilder says to the shoeshine boy, "Pardon me, boy, is this the Transylvania station?" and the boy (Peter Halton) answers, "Ya, track 29! Say, can I give you a shine?" And everyone has a favorite sight gag, whether it's Igor's constantly shifting hump or the ravishing of Elizabeth by the monster (his "enormous schwanstucker" transforms her into a sex-crazed "bride of Frankenstein"). I think it's safe to say that nearly everyone loves *Young Frankenstein*, which was selected for preservation by the Library of Congress National Film Registry in 2003 for showcasing the range and diversity of American film heritage.

In a 2006 interview, Gerald Hirschfeld revealed the following: "I happen to have a very close personal friend who's got two children; they're now in their teens, but at the time they may have been eight or ten or twelve years old, something like that. They bought a videotape of *Young Frankenstein* and they wore it out. They knew the lines, they knew all the gag lines . . . and these were young kids, and they could relate to the story of *Young Frankenstein* even though they might not have ever seen the original *Frankenstein*; they probably hadn't."

Gruskoff pointed out that people still came up to him and said, "You made that movie?" and they started giving him lines from it. Why is it that the film remains so popular?

Wilder had his own idea about why *Young Frankenstein* still resonates:

> I think the thing that makes Frankenstein live as a concept—Mary Shelley's *Frankenstein*—it's about a creature that's formed who has love in his heart, who wants to be loved and is misunderstood. It's a classic theme. People have tried it in other ways, but it's always worked best, I think in the Frankenstein frame. And even though we were doing a comedy—a ridiculous comedy—that classic theme is still there. And I think that's why it [*Young Frankenstein*] lives.

In *Young Frankenstein: The Story of the Making of the Film*, Brooks wrote, "Of all my films, I am the proudest of this one. We set out to make a beautiful period picture, with all the craftsmanship of James Whale's 1930s films. And, of course, this time with laughs. My hope was that *Young Frankenstein* would transport audiences the way I was transported as a kid sitting in the dark in Williamsburg. I think we succeeded."

Young Frankenstein is indeed Brooks's crowning achievement as director; *Blazing Saddles* may indeed be the funnier film, but *Young Frankenstein* is more polished and heartfelt. It may be best described with a word that's rarely used to describe any film, much less a comedy: simply put, *Young Frankenstein* is a masterpiece.

12

"PUTTIN' ON THE RITZ"

As was the case with *Blazing Saddles* before it, *Young Frankenstein* became an instant cultural touchstone. Phrases such as "Abby Normal" and "There wolf, there castle" were being parroted by fans the world over. Perhaps the most noticeable aftereffect of its popularity, however, was the fact that it killed off serious Frankenstein movies for a decade or more.

In fact, history was repeating itself: after *Abbott and Costello Meet Frankenstein* was released in 1948, there were no serious attempts at making a movie with the name "Frankenstein" in it until British producers Hammer Films unleashed *The Curse of Frankenstein* in 1957. Released in the United States by Warner Bros., the film was a box-office sensation and made international stars out of Peter Cushing (Baron Frankenstein) and Christopher Lee (the Creature). *The Curse of Frankenstein* single-handedly revived the gothic horror genre and opened the floodgates for such low-budget imitations as *I Was a Teenage Frankenstein* that same year and *Frankenstein's Daughter* and *Frankenstein 1970* in the following year.

Hammer carried on with a whole series of Frankenstein films: *The Revenge of Frankenstein* (1958), *The Evil of Frankenstein* (1964), *Frankenstein Created Woman* (1967), *Frankenstein Must Be Destroyed* (1969), *The Horror of Frankenstein* (1970, and the only one not starring Cushing), and *Frankenstein and the Monster from Hell* (1974). Much as the Abbott and Costello movie killed off the Universal horror cycle in 1948 for a decade, *Young Frankenstein* did the same for the Hammer cycle. Mary Shelley's story was in the public domain; anyone could have filmed it again, but there was only one more attempt in the 1970s, a low-budget Irish/Swedish adaptation of the novel written and directed by Calvin Floyd, starring Stanley Kubrick's protégé Leon Vitali as Frankenstein and Swedish actor Per Oscarsson as his creation. The film, originally titled *Victor Frankenstein*, barely received a release in the United States under the title *Terror of Frankenstein* in 1977, and few fans saw it until its video release in the 1980s. One of the more faithful adaptations of the novel, it remains a well-produced, well-acted failure.

It wasn't until 1985 that another attempt was made to mine Shelley's work, and interestingly enough, the name "Frankenstein" was not used: *The Bride* was released by Columbia Pictures, starring pop singer Sting as Baron Frankenstein, Clancy Brown as his male creation, and Jennifer Beals (*Flashdance*, 1983) as his female creation. Although nicely filmed in European locations, it was a critical and box-office bomb.

In the early 1990s, there was a Frankenstein renaissance of sorts. Cult director Roger Corman (*Pit and the Pendulum*, 1961) contributed *Frankenstein Unbound* (1990), with Raul Julia as Dr. Frankenstein and Nick Brimble as the monster. Again, it was not a great box-office success. That same year, Frank Henenlotter's *Frankenhooker* became an R-rated cult item, a black comedy about a medical school dropout

(James Lorinz) who stitches together parts of dead prostitutes to create a grotesque creature (Patty Mullen). On a more serious note, Turner Network Television's *Frankenstein* (1992) starred Patrick Bergin and Randy Quaid in a direct adaptation of Shelley's novel.

The big adaptation, however, was *Mary Shelley's Frankenstein* (1994), directed by Kenneth Branagh, who also played Frankenstein, with none other than Robert De Niro as his creation. Although critically panned for the most part, the film—a follow-up of sorts to the success of *Bram Stoker's Dracula*, directed by Francis Ford Coppola in 1992—raked in a worldwide total of $112 million at the box office.

And so, exactly twenty years after *Young Frankenstein*, Shelley's novel was treated seriously again, and ten years after that, an even more faithful adaptation was made as a television miniseries for the Hallmark Channel directed by Kevin Connor (*From Beyond the Grave, 1973*) and starring Alec Newman and Luke Goss. And, as of this writing, horror specialist Guillermo Del Toro (*Pan's Labyrinth*, 2006) is preparing yet another big-budget version of the original novel.

In addition to an array of low-budget films such as *The Frankenstein Syndrome* (2010) and *Frankenstein's Army* (2013)—Shelley's novel is in the public domain, after all—more recent high-profile adaptations have included *I, Frankenstein* (2014), starring Aaron Eckhart and Bill Nighy, and *Victor Frankenstein* (2015) with Daniel Radcliffe and James McAvoy.

The reason for this rather brisk recap of the history of "serious" Frankenstein films since 1974 is this: despite one or two of them having huge budgets ($45 million for *Mary Shelley's* Frankenstein) and big stars (Sting, De Niro, etc.), none of them so far is nearly as well-remembered as *Young Frankenstein*. The fact is, many people who would never ordinarily watch a "serious" Frankenstein movie have seen *Young Frankenstein*, and indeed some younger viewers may never have seen any other versions. Brooks and company made a film that became almost instantly iconic, and it has remained that way for the past fifty years.

There have been other comic versions as well: *Billy Frankenstein* (1998), from director Fred Olen Ray, who also made *Bikini Frankenstein* (2010); *Rock 'n' Roll Frankenstein* (1999), in which the monster is created from the remains of Jimi Hendrix, Buddy Holly, Sid Vicious, and Elvis Presley; and even computer-animated spoofs such as the *Hotel Transylvania* franchise beginning in 2012. Again, though, none of these films have had anything like the impact of *Young Frankenstein*, which stands nearly alone in the pantheon of Frankenstein parodies; in fact, the only film that comes close to it in name recognition is the legendary *Abbott and Costello Meet Frankenstein*.

Thanks to countless TV broadcasts, Brooks's movie has stayed in the public consciousness since 1974. It was released to DVD in 1998, reissued in that format in 2006 and for a third time in 2004 (as well as on Blu-ray for the first time) for the film's fortieth anniversary. It remains hugely popular in home media—but that's not all.

In 2001, a musical comedy version of *The Producers* opened on Broadway. Adapted by Brooks (along with Thomas Meehan) from his 1967 movie, the show starred Nathan Lane and Matthew Broderick and ran for 2,502 performances, winning an amazing twelve Tony Awards. The show's success led to a successful British production in London's West End that ran for over two years. And, just to prove that what goes around comes around, it also spawned a 2005 film version starring Lane and Broderick.

After that Broadway blockbuster, Brooks decided to adapt another of his films for the stage, so he got together with Meehan in 2006 to start work on a musical version of *Young Frankenstein*. A pre-Broadway tryout in Seattle and four weeks of previews led to a Broadway opening on November 8, 2007. The monster had been revived, and this time *Young Frankenstein* was directed by Susan Stroman, who had also directed *The Producers* for the stage, and the production starred Roger Bart as Dr. Frankenstein, Megan Mullally as Elizabeth, Christopher Fitzgerald as Igor, Andrea Martin as Frau Blucher, Sutton Foster as Inga, Shuler Hensley as the monster, and Fred Applegate as Inspector Kemp. Originally, it was hoped that Cloris Leachman would reprise her role as Frau Blucher, but because of concerns over her age (she was eighty at the time), she was replaced by *Second City Television* alumnus Martin.

The opulent sets for the production were designed by Robin Wagner, while the costumes were designed by William Ivey Long. The musical reportedly cost upward of $16 million to produce; the cost of the original movie thirty years previously was around $2 million. There are numerous differences between the film and the stage version, aside from the musical numbers. Elizabeth arrives in Transylvania earlier than she does in the film, the scene with the monster and the little girl is not retained in the musical, and the show features the villagers attempting to hang Frederick before he's saved by the monster.

The Broadway show is virtually wall-to-wall music, featuring such numbers as "Roll in the Hay," "He Vas My Boyfriend," and, of course, "Puttin' on the Ritz." The orchestrations by Doug Besterman were for a twenty-four-piece orchestra, while the London performances were scaled down to a ten-piece orchestra.

Unlike those for *The Producers*, the reviews for the Broadway version of *Young Frankenstein* were mixed. In the *New York Times*, critic Ben Brantley called it "an overblown burlesque review," while Clive Barnes of the *New York Post* found the show "nearly very good indeed" and praised Brooks and Stroman for "pull[ing] out every stop." The London version received more positive reviews, although Charles Spencer, writing in the *Daily Telegraph*, compared it unfavorably to *The Producers*, complaining that "the show fatally lacks that touch of the sublime that made *The Producers* so special."

Otherwise, *Young Frankenstein*—the musical—received four- to five-star ratings in such British publications as the *Guardian* and *London Evening Standard*. This may have been because the West End version, which didn't open until 2017, was "revised." Whatever the case, the musical version of *Young Frankenstein* (with music and lyrics by Brooks himself and the book by Meehan) didn't quite replicate the success of *The Producers* musical, although it ran for 484 performances on Broadway and for eleven months in the West End, which is no small accomplishment. It won no Tony Awards (although it was nominated for three), although it did win a Broadway.com Audience Award for Favorite New Broadway Musical.

In an online interview by Jackie Loohauis-Bennett, Brooks pointed out how delighted he was with the audience reaction to the show: "I love what they do," he said. "The audience knows *Young Frankenstein*, the movie; they didn't know *The Producers*. They all neigh when anyone onstage says, "Frau Blucher." And they can't wait for the blind hermit to spill the hot soup on the monster's lap. It's great to see the audience play ping-pong with the actors."

The show was successful enough to spawn two recordings: the original cast album, which was released by Decca Records in 2007, which became #3 on the Billboard Cast Album Chart early in 2008; and the Original London Cast Recording, which was released in 2018. There were also plans for a live broadcast event on the ABC Network during the last quarter of 2020, with Brooks himself producing. Unfortunately, the live broadcast was scrapped due to the COVID-19 pandemic. As of this writing, there's no further word on the project.

There were two national tours of the show, one in 2010 and the other in 2011. The revised UK production made its American debut in 2022, starring A. J. Holmes as Dr. Frankenstein, Sarah Wolter as Elizabeth, Maggie Ek as Inga, Trent Mills as the monster, Wesley Slade as Igor, Sally Struthers as Frau Blucher, and Joe Hart as Inspector Kemp and the hermit. It premiered at the La Mirada Theatre for the Performing Arts in La Mirada, California, in September of that year.

The key to the success of the musical version lies in what Brooks said in his online interview: the audience knew the movie, and anticipated what the actors would do in the stage production. Brooks knew that he couldn't vary the plot too much, because it would disappoint the fans of the film. It was just another example of how iconic and beloved the film had become in the intervening years.

Epilogue: Fifty Years On

After the fantastic success of *Blazing Saddles* and *Young Frankenstein*, Brooks and Wilder went their separate ways. The first past the post with a solo feature was Wilder, who had come up with an idea for a musical comedy about the brother of Sherlock Holmes. He wrote a screenplay for what became his directorial debut, *The Adventure of Sherlock Holmes' Smarter Brother* (1975). After the wonderful time they all had on *Young Frankenstein*, Wilder had no trouble convincing Marty Feldman and Madeline Kahn to join the cast, which included Dom DeLuise, Roy Kinnear, and Leo McKern, with Douglas Wilmer, who had previously starred in the BBC series *Sherlock Holmes* and Thorley Walters, who had played Dr. Watson in three feature films, reprising their roles for the movie.

The Adventure of Sherlock Holmes' Smarter Brother was well received at the time, with Vincent Canby of the *New York Times* calling it "a charming slapstick comedy" and Charles Champlin of the *Los Angeles Times* dubbing it "a kindly and ingratiating trip through Holmes' sweet home as it never was." Of all Wilder's directorial efforts, the movie comes the closest to recapturing some of the magic of *Young*

Frankenstein in its comic absurdity, sweetness, and obvious affection for the source material.

As for Brooks, feeling audacious because of his heady successes, he decided to make the first silent comedy since Charlie Chaplin. *Silent Movie* (1976) was the result, written by Brooks, Ron Clark, Rudy De Luca, and Barry Levinson, with Brooks in his first starring role. The supporting cast was a "who's who" of comedy at that time, including Feldman, DeLuise, and Sid Caesar, and the non-comic actors (most of whom played cameo roles) included Burt Reynolds, Paul Newman, James Caan, Liza Minnelli, and Brooks's wife, Anne Bancroft. Lacking the participation of Madeline Kahn or Teri Garr, the sexpot role in this one was more than adequately portrayed by Broadway star Bernadette Peters, her first of many such film roles. One of the more amusing jokes in the movie was provided by mime Marcel Marceau, uttering the only word in the picture: "Non!"

Roger Ebert of the *Chicago Sun-Times* praised *Silent Movie*, referring to it as "not only funny, but fun." He felt that it was equal to *Blazing Saddles* and superior to *Young Frankenstein*, although it didn't quite do the box-office business of either film, nevertheless grossing a healthy $36.15 million.

Ebert was one of the first critics to recognize Brooks as a "celebrity director," joining the pantheon of such filmmakers as Hitchcock, Orson Welles, and Steven Spielberg, among other such heady names. He wrote in his review, "Mel Brooks will do anything for a laugh. Anything. He has no shame. He's an anarchist; his movies inhabit a universe in which everything is possible and the outrageous is probable, and *Silent Movie*, where Brooks has taken a considerable stylistic risk and pulled it off triumphantly, made me laugh a lot. On the Brooks-Laff-O-Meter, I laughed more than in *Young Frankenstein* and about as much as in *Blazing Saddles*, although not, I confess, as much as in *The Producers*."

Silent Movie featured the first on-screen pairing of Brooks and Bancroft; they had been married since 1964. Bancroft had had an uncredited cameo as a member of the congregation in *Blazing Saddles*, but *Silent Movie* was the first time they acted together. They later costarred in Brooks's remake of *To Be or Not to Be* (1983), and Bancroft had another cameo in *Dracula: Dead and Loving It* just before she passed away in 2005.

In a 1981 episode of *The Tonight Show Starring Johnny Carson*, guest Alan Alda told Carson that he had attended the premiere of *Silent Movie* in Westwood, where Brooks and Bancroft were in attendance. He said that he most likely laughed harder than anyone else in the audience; and, after the movie, he complimented Brooks and Bancroft on how much the movie had made him laugh. Alda said that Bancroft, with perfect comic timing, retorted, "Oh, was that you laughing? You see, Mel? I told you *some* idiot would find this funny!"

Wilder was finding his own niche when his agent sent him a script for a movie called *Super Chief*. Wilder accepted a leading role in the film, but he also felt that another major role should be filled by none other than Richard Pryor. A comedy-thriller that had strong echoes of Hitchcock's *North by Northwest*, *Super Chief* ultimately became *Silver Streak* (1976), and was the first teaming of many for Wilder and Pryor, who, in essence, became the first interracial comedy team. Directed by Arthur Hiller (*The Americanization of Emily*, 1964), *Silver Streak* became a critical and box-office success, and much of that success was due to the chemistry between Wilder and Pryor.

The writer of *Silver Streak*, Colin Higgins, later claimed that the producers initially balked at the idea of casting the volatile Pryor, and that producers Thomas L. Miller and Edward K. Milkis had considered casting another black actor as backup. Ultimately, though, they caved to Wilder's wishes and, after being cast, Pryor was by all accounts totally professional during production.

And so both Brooks and Wilder were riding high—separately—during the mid-1970s. Branching off into different directions, Wilder made three more comedies with Pryor, while Brooks continued his run of parodies, with Hitchcock himself his next "target."

Written once again by Brooks, Clark, De Luca, and Levinson, *High Anxiety* (1977), its title a takeoff on Hitchcock's *Vertigo* (1958), was the first movie that Brooks produced on his own. It starred the director/producer in another lead role, along with key support from Madeline Kahn, Cloris Leachman, Harvey Korman, Ron Carey, Dick Van Patten, and Howard Morris. In this film, Brooks managed to satirize not only *Vertigo*, but *Psycho* (1960), *The Birds* (1963), *Suspicion* (1941), *Spellbound* (1945), *Dial M for Murder* (1954), and *North by Northwest* (1959), among many other Hitchcock films and tropes. Brooks cast himself as Dr. Richard H. (for Harpo) Thorndyke, a psychologist who suffers from "high anxiety" despite winning a Nobel Prize.

High Anxiety was not quite as well received as the previous three films, with Vincent Canby of the *New York Times* opining, "[*High Anxiety*] is as witty and as disciplined as *Young Frankenstein*, though it has one built-in problem: Hitchcock himself is a very funny man. . . . Being so self-aware, Hitchcock's films deny an easy purchase to the parodist, especially one who admires the subject the way Mr. Brooks does. There's nothing to send up, really."

Roger Ebert concurred: whereas he had given *Silent Movie* a four-star rating, he only gave two and a half stars to *High Anxiety*. In his review for the *Chicago Sun-Times*, he wrote, "One of the problems with Mel Brooks's *High Anxiety* is that it picks a tricky target: It's a spoof of the works of Alfred Hitchcock, but Hitchcock's films are often funny themselves. And satire works best when its target is self-important. It's easy for the *National Lampoon* to take on the *Reader's Digest*. But can you imagine a satire of the *National Lampoon*?"

Ebert finished by writing, "Brooks has made a specialty of movie satires: *Blazing Saddles*, *Young Frankenstein* and *Silent Movie*. But they took on well-chosen targets. It's one thing to kid the self-conscious seriousness of a western or a horror movie. It's another to take on a director of such sophistication that half the audience won't even get the in-jokes the other half is laughing at."

The box-office for *High Anxiety* was slightly more positive than its critical reception, although under the three previous hits, coming in at $31.6 million. Despite its lukewarm reception, Hitchcock himself was very pleased with it, and, as a token of his appreciation, he sent Brooks a case of wine—knowing that Brooks was something of a connoisseur—with a note dated March 1, 1978, that read,

My dear Mel,

What a splendid entertainment, one that should give you no anxieties of any kind.

I thank you most humbly for your dedication and I offer you further thanks on behalf of the Golden Gate Bridge.

With kindest regards and again my warmest congratulations,

Hitch

High Anxiety turned out to be the start of something new for Brooks. With an assistant producer named Stuart Cornfeld, Brooks decided to mount his own production company, Brooksfilms. He decided that the name was neutral enough so that audiences wouldn't necessarily expect a full-blown comedy, as he wanted to branch out into different types of films. His first film under this banner was *Fatso*, written by his wife, Anne.

With Bancroft directing and starring (along with Dom DeLuise and Ron Carey), *Fatso* (1980) was neither a box-office nor a critical success. A romantic comedy quite unlike the films directed by Brooks, *Fatso* turned out to be an inauspicious debut for both Bancroft as director and for Brooksfilms.

Undaunted, Brooks moved onto his next project, *The Elephant Man*, a 1980 biographical drama based on the life of Joseph Merrick (called John Merrick in the film), a grotesquely deformed man who lived in Victorian London. Directed by David Lynch (*Eraserhead*, 1977), *The Elephant Man* turned out to be a huge success and was nominated for eight Academy Awards, including for Best Director and Best Actor (John Hurt). It ended up not winning any, but it received considerable critical acclaim and did good box-office, grossing $26 million in the United States alone. Like *Young Frankenstein*, it was photographed in black and white, this time by renowned British cinematographer and director Freddie Francis, who had already won an Academy Award for photographing *Sons and Lovers* (1960).

Despite producing more serious fare, by 1980, Siskel and Ebert, on their eponymous television show, declared Mel Brooks and Woody Allen (the latter of whom was also starting to direct more dramatic films) as "[t]he two most successful comedy directors in the world today . . . America's two funniest filmmakers." Perhaps because of this accolade, Brooks decided to return to directing with the outrageously titled *History of the World, Part I* (1981). Brooks decided that the only types of movies left to spoof were historical spectacles and Biblical epics, so he combined the two in *History of the World, Part I*, which was a parodic look at mankind from the Stone Age through the French Revolution. Brooks once again wrote, produced, and directed, with narration by none other than Orson Welles.

Brooks's latest comedy received mixed reviews and was a modest success at the box office, grossing $31.7 million, which was considered something of a disappointment. Mind you, the competition on opening weekend was tough: *Raiders of the Lost Ark* and *Clash of the Titans*, with the public in the mood for fantasy. Brooks's movie also came in behind *Cheech and Chong's Nice Dreams*, which was the biggest comedy of that summer weekend. Added to that embarrassment, however, poor word of mouth also impacted the box office of *History of the World, Part I*. It was something of a decline for Brooks, not only in commercial success, but in quality.

Brooks blamed the relative failure of his new movie on the new regime at 20th Century Fox—Alan Ladd Jr. was out, despite the fact that he had greenlit *Star Wars*—and Brooks had a contract dispute with Fox over foreign distribution. Brooksfilms ended up taking the foreign rights. As for Ladd, he had resigned of his own accord after having a disagreement with the new bosses, and he ended up becoming the head of MGM. Brooksfilms became the overseas distributor of *History of the World, Part I* and ended up producing the well-received *My Favorite Year* in 1982, a delightful comedy starring Peter O'Toole and directed by Richard Benjamin that, for inspiration, hearkened back to Brooks's experiences with Sid Caesar. It was released by MGM.

On a more serious note, Brooksfilms went from strength to strength with *Frances* (1982), the life story of ill-fated actress Frances Farmer, who rose to fame in the 1930s before having a nervous breakdown and being hospitalized against her will. In the movie *Frances*, released by Universal, the title role was played by Jessica Lange, who was nominated for an Oscar for her performance. Ironically, she didn't win for that film, but she did win the same year for her supporting role in *Tootsie*, in which she costarred with Dustin Hoffman. In any case, Brooksfilms was quickly gaining a reputation as a production company dedicated to high-quality filmmaking.

Brooks's disagreement with Fox was short-lived: his next movie as producer (but not director) for the studio was *To Be or Not to Be*, a remake of the 1942 Jack Benny/Carole Lombard comedy that had been directed by Ernst Lubitsch. After the relative failure of *History of the World, Part I*, Brooks decided to let another director, Alan Johnson, take the helm on this new and rather different venture, in which he and Bancroft would take the roles once played by Benny and Lombard.

Essentially a musical comedy version of the original, *To Be or Not to Be* was successful at the box office and garnered some excellent reviews as well. Vincent Canby wrote in the *New York Times*, "Everybody can relax. Mel Brooks's remake of Ernst Lubitsch's 1942 classic *To Be or Not to Be* is smashingly funny. . . . It's no news that Mr. Brooks is a national treasure. The revelation for film audiences is that Miss Bancroft is such a wildly gifted comedienne. . . . Performing singly or in tandem, they are terrific."

In 1985, Brooks brought back his cinematographer Freddie Francis from *The Elephant Man*, this time to direct a film called *The Doctor and the Devils*, based on a screenplay that Dylan Thomas had written in the 1950s. It told the true story of Burke and Hare, who robbed graves in Edinburgh, Scotland, during the 1840s to supply their benefactor, Dr. Knox, with cadavers used in his medical research—which was, at the time, quite illegal. Although the names were changed in the screenplay, the film was fairly historically accurate, with future James Bond Timothy Dalton playing Dr. Knox (here called Dr. Rock), and Jonathan Pryce and Stephen Rea as the Burke and Hare characters. Dylan's original screenplay was adapted by playwright and screenwriter Ronald Harwood.

In between his stints as cinematographer during the early 1960s and 1980s, Francis had directed some of the best British horror films of the era, such as *The Skull* (1960), *Dracula Has Risen from the Grave* (1968), and *Tales from the Crypt* (1972). Brooks hired him to direct *The Doctor and the Devils* both because of those credits and because he had done such a sterling job photographing *The Elephant Man*.

Although it was splendidly produced and rich in period atmosphere, *The Doctor and the Devils* ended up falling between two schools—not enough horror for genre fans but too grim for mainstream viewers. As a result, it failed to find an audience and received decidedly mixed reviews, with Vincent Canby praising its "first-rate English cast," while opining that, "Mr. [Ronald] Harwood's screenplay, which retains a lot of the original Thomas dialogue, is much more fun to see than the Thomas screenplay is to read."

One of the biggest hits from Brooksfilms was David Cronenberg's 1986 remake of the 1958 sci-fi/horror film *The Fly*, the original having starred Al (David) Hedison, Vincent Price, and Patricia Owens. The new version starred Jeff Goldblum, John Getz, and Geena Davis and was only loosely based on the original film, which in turn was adapted from a short story by George Langelaan.

Cronenberg, known as a director of "body horror" movies such as *Shivers* (1975), *Scanners* (1981), and *Videodrome* (1983), turned out to be the perfect choice to direct *The Fly*, which he invested with some genuinely disturbing and queasy moments. Almost more of Franz Kafka's *Metamorphosis* than a straight horror film, Cronenberg's *The Fly* grossed—and I do mean "grossed"—over $60 million worldwide, received generally positive reviews, and won an Academy Award for Best Makeup by Chris Walas and Stephan Dupuis. Many critics felt that Goldlblum should have been nominated for Best Actor, but this didn't occur, with Gene Siskel opining that Goldblum "got stiffed" because the Academy rarely honored horror films with such accolades—despite them having given Best Actor to Fredric March for *Dr. Jekyll and Mr. Hyde* (1931) and Best Actress to Sissy Spacek for *Carrie* (1976). Nevertheless, *The Fly* was another huge success for Brooksfilms, and it begot a sequel, *The Fly II* (1986), directed by Chris Walas himself.

Brooks directed only one other comedy during the 1980s, a takeoff on *Star Wars* called *Spaceballs* (1987). Along the way, the movie also poked fun at other sci-fi epics such as *Alien* (1979), *2001: A Space Odyssey*, *Planet of the Apes* (both 1968), and even *The Wizard of Oz* (1939). *Spaceballs* starred Bill Pullman, Daphne Zuniga, John Candy, Rick Moranis, Dick Van Patten—and the voice of Joan Rivers for its robot character, Dot Matrix. The movie, written by Brooks, Ronny Graham, and Thomas Meehan, also featured cameos by Brooks regulars Dom DeLuise and Rudy De Luca.

Although it has since acquired a cult reputation, *Spaceballs* did only okay business and received mixed reviews at the time of its release. Roger Ebert wrote, "I enjoyed a lot of the movie, but I kept thinking I was at a revival. The strangest thing about *Spaceballs* is that it should have been made several years ago, before our appetite for *Star Wars* satires had been completely exhausted."

Ebert went on to make a cogent observation: "The earlier ones are stronger than the most recent films, and I keep wishing Brooks would satirize something current and tricky, like the John Hughes teenage films, instead of picking on old targets. With *Spaceballs*, he has made the kind of movie that doesn't really need a Mel Brooks." *Variety* was even more pointed: "Mel Brooks will do anything for a laugh. Unfortunately, what he does in *Spaceballs*, a misguided parody of the *Star Wars* adventures, isn't very funny."

On a $22.7 million budget, *Spaceballs* only managed to bring in $38,119,483 at the box office. It even managed to win the 1987 "Stinkers Bad Movie Award" for Worst Picture, over such contenders as *The Garbage Pail Kids Movie*, *Ishtar*, *Leonard Part 6*, and *Who's That Girl?* The question in 1987 seemed to be this: was Mel Brooks losing his mojo?

In 1989, Brooks went back to his roots in television to produce a series called *The Nutt House*, starring Harvey Korman and Cloris Leachman. It was a broad farce—no surprise there—about a hotel in New York City that has fallen on hard times. Sadly, it also felt like Brooks had fallen on hard times, and only six episodes of the eleven that were filmed were broadcast before NBC canceled the series.

Brooks's next film as director was *Life Stinks* in 1991, which didn't fare much better. Although Ebert called it "a warm-hearted comedy," the film lost money at the box office, bringing in only $4.1 million in the United States and Canada against its $13 million budget. Instead of going from strength to strength, it appeared that Brooks was going from loss to loss at this stage in his career.

Things brightened up considerably with Brooks's next directorial effort, *Robin Hood: Men in Tights* (1993). In this case, Brooks was belatedly taking Ebert's advice and parodying something current, the highly successful *Robin Hood: Prince of Thieves* (1991), starring Kevin Costner in the title role. There are also strong elements of the classic Hollywood treatment of the story *The Adventures of Robin Hood* (1938), starring Errol Flynn.

With Cary Elwes (*The Princess Bride*, 1987) as Robin Hood—who at one point makes fun of Costner's lack of a British accent—*Robin Hood: Men in Tights* is in good hands, and it brings back some of that old Brooks magic. Written by Brooks, Evan Chandler, and J. David Shapiro, the movie has an anything-goes, free-wheeling charm that is hard to resist. Richard Lewis as King John, Roger Rees as the Sheriff of Nottingham, and Tracey Ullman as a witch called Latrine all add to the fun; and there's a scene with Dom DeLuise that's one of the funniest in the film, along with cameos including Patrick Stewart as King Richard, Dick Van Patten as an abbot, Chuck McCann as a villager, and Brooks himself as "Rabbi Tuckman."

Reviews were mixed, with Vincent Canby of the *New York Times* pointing out the following: "What's missing is the kind of densely packed comic screenplay that helped to make *Young Frankenstein* and *High Anxiety* two of the most delectable movie parodies of the past 20 years"; while Rita Kempley of the *Washington Post* called it "[a] point-less and untimely lampoon of *Robin Hood: Prince of Thieves* from the increasingly creaky spoofmeister Mel Brooks."

Whatever the critics thought, *Robin Hood: Men in Tights* did good business, bringing in a worldwide total of $72 million, making it Brooks's fifth highest-grossing movie. Fox was reportedly so pleased with its performance that they (along with the French company Gaumont, who cofinanced it) bankrolled *Dracula: Dead and Loving It*, which co-screenwriter Steve Haberman (with Brooks and Rudy De Luca) has already discussed in his interview for this book. Essentially a parody of Tod Browning's *Dracula* (1931) starring Bela Lugosi, *Dracula: Dead and Loving It* also spoofs Terence Fisher's *Horror of Dracula* (1958), Roman Polanski's *The Fearless Vampire Killers* (1967), and Francis Ford Coppola's recent *Bram Stoker's Dracula* (1992).

Starring Leslie Nielsen, who had in the last decade become a comedy icon in such parodies as *Airplane!* (1980) and *The Naked Gun: From the Files of Police Squad!* (1988), *Dracula: Dead and Loving It* costarred Brooks as Professor Van Helsing, Peter MacNicol as Renfield, Steven Weber as Jonathan Harker, Lysette Anthony as Lucy, and Amy Yasbeck (who had played Maid Marian in *Robin Hood: Men in Tights)* as Mina. Harvey Korman came back to the Brooks fold to play Dr. Seward.

Reviews were mostly negative. Joe Leydon wrote in *Variety*, "Leslie Nielsen toplines to agreeable effect as Count Dracula. . . . Trouble is, while *Dead and Loving It* earns its fair share of grins and giggles, it never really cuts loose and goes for the belly laughs. . . . The only real sparks are set off by MacNicol as Renfield, the solicitor who develops a taste for flies and spiders after being bitten by Dracula."

Steve Haberman recalled a disagreement between him and Brooks on *Dracula: Dead and Loving It* that was reminiscent of the debate between Brooks and Wilder on the "Puttin' on the Ritz" scene in *Young Frankenstein*:

> During pre-production on *Dracula*, I met Christopher Lee for the first time and he was very, very nice. Some people said he was cold, but I didn't find him that way at all. And everyone had loaded me down with material for him to sign. And I was there with an artist friend of mine with a bunch of things for him to sign . . . and he signed them all, and my stuff too. . . . And we were talking about Dracula, as one does with Christopher Lee, and he said, "You must realize that I have never made fun of the character." And I said, "Well, it may interest you to know that I'm working on a parody with Mel Brooks called *Dracula: Dead and Loving It*." And he did that gesture with his hand, you know, where he just sort of waves it in the air. Just very dismissive.
>
> The next day, I came into the office and the secretary said to me, "Steve, did you meet Christopher Lee yesterday?" I said, "Yes, I did." She said, "His agent called this morning and said he'd be interested in being in *Dracula*." So I told Mel I had an idea.
>
> This was my idea that I pitched to Mel: Christopher Lee plays the graverobber that Lucy kills. Mel was pals with Frank Langella, so we'd get him to play a part. And we'll ask Gary Oldman to play a part. And we CGI [computer-generated imagery] Bela Lugosi into the movie! Four actors

who famously played Dracula! And Mel goes, "I gotta think about this. Let me think about it."

So we go to lunch and we don't talk about it, and we come back and I said, "So, what do you think? Should we call Christopher Lee?" And Mel said, "No, we're not gonna do that." I said, "Why?" He said, "It's too self-conscious." I said, "We're making a parody! What's more self-conscious than a parody? Let's go for it." And he said, "I don't want to do it, it breaks it."

I have a million stories of stuff like that that Mel said no to. And I'm sure he does as well. Sometimes I said no to Mel! I'd say, "No, come on, Mel, that's stupid." Or I'd say, "Let's not say anything about Nazis or Jews." And he went with it, he was okay. It's a collaboration.

I asked Haberman if he was happy with the way *Dracula: Dead and Loving It* turned out. "Up to a point, yeah," he responded.

I mean, there are things . . . look, when you write a script and then you rewrite the script and then you cast the script and then you cut the script and go to fifteen screenings and cut this out and move this over here and change that music cue and stuff like that, you completely lose perspective. If I never see those movies again, I'll be thrilled, you know? It's not that I don't like them, it's just that that was your life for a couple of years. I think that now *Dracula: Dead and Loving It* has a cult as well. A lot of people say to me that it's their favorite Halloween movie and they watch it every Halloween, which is all I really wanted to do.

When I was a kid, every Halloween they showed *Abbott and Costello Meet Frankenstein*. They showed it at four o'clock in the afternoon, so that by 5:30 when it got dark, you could go trick or treating. I thought that the movie gods figured that out when I was a kid, because it was so perfect. You watch *Abbott and Costello Meet Frankenstein*, get in your costume, and you go trick or treating. That's the kind of movie I wanted to make. Now that you can watch any movie you want any time you want, so many people say to me, "My movie on Halloween is *Dracula: Dead and Loving It*." And that makes me feel really good.

Haberman said he was responsible for many of the Hammer references in his *Dracula:*

> I showed Mel *Horror of Dracula* (1958). I remember I showed it to him in his office and his secretary said, "That's very serious music [in the film]!" I said, "This is just getting you into the mood for this. Wait until you see the first shot!"
>
> When it was done, Mel said, "It's too pastel." I said, "What do you mean?" He goes, "The color! It's too pastel!" I said, "But you know what? We're parodying the Lucy staking scene, we're parodying the ending with the daylight, we're doing a lot of that."

I told Haberman how much I enjoyed the scene in *Dracula: Dead and Loving It* with Lucy (Lysette Anthony), in which she attempts to seduce Jonathan Harker (Steve Weber) into vampirism. Weber tries to resist, saying, "I'm British!" and, in response, Anthony cups her rather ample breasts and shouts, "So are these!"

"That was me and Mel," Haberman said.

> "I'm British," was mine and "So are these" was Mel's. You know, Mel didn't want to do the blood scene (of Lucy's staking). That was like the "Puttin' on the Ritz" scene; he said it was too much, crossing the line, it was too disgusting. So you know what I did? I had the casting girl go out at lunchtime and get a VHS of *Evil Dead 2*. And I cued up the scene where Bruce Campbell cuts his hand off. And when we came back from lunch, I said to Mel, "I want you to watch something," and I showed him that scene. He was laughing his ass off all through it, and he said, "I get it, I get it now." I said, "See? Bad taste can be funny!" Imagine me telling Mel Brooks that bad taste can be funny!

Haberman went on to say that *Horror of Dracula*—the first Hammer version starring Christopher Lee in the role—is his favorite Dracula movie. "That's my favorite one," he continued,

> but the structure of it does not lend itself to comedy. If you start with Harker coming to Castle Dracula and getting killed at the end of the first act, you can't really be funny after that. But if you start with Renfield, as we did, going to Castle Dracula and he becomes a fly-eating lunatic, then you've got some comedy on your hands. I think the more horror references you know, the more you like it.

In my book *Comedy Horror Films: A Chronological History, 1914–2008*, I took pains to defend the film, writing, "It ranks with Polanski's *The Fearless Vampire Killers* as one of the greatest vampire comedies ever made." I was a voice in the wilderness, however.

Sadly, the movie was unfairly compared to *Young Frankenstein*—a very high bar indeed—and it was unsuccessful both critically and commercially, although it too has acquired a cult reputation over the years. Film buffs such as yours truly certainly appreciated the in-jokes, but apparently most audiences didn't, as it made only $10.7 million back on its $30 million budget.

Dracula: Dead and Loving It was Brooks's last film (to date) as director. Since 2001, Brooks has returned to the Broadway stage with great success. As previously noted, his musical adaptation of *The Producers* was met with critical acclaim and great success at the box office. It led directly to the 2005 film remake directed by Susan Stroman.

In 2006, the musical stage adaptation of *Young Frankenstein* opened on Broadway at the Hilton Theater (now the Lyric Theater), earning mixed reviews from critics but doing well with the patrons. Beginning in 2008, Brooks was involved in the production of a TV sequel to *Spaceballs* called *Spaceballs: The Animated Series*, which ran for thirteen episodes on G4 and Canada's Super Channel. In the animated arena, Brooks has provided voices for various characters in such series as *Robots* and in animated feature films such as *Mr. Peabody and Sherman* (2014), *Hotel Transylvania 2* (2015), and *Hotel Transylvania 3: Summer Vacation* (2018).

Brooks has teased and joked about adapting *Blazing Saddles* as a stage musical, but thus far nothing has come of it. Two significant developments did occur in 2021, however; Brooks released his autobiography

All About Me, and he signed to write and produce *History of the World, Part II*, a "sequel" to his 1981 film as a series on Hulu. And, for his latest accolade, he received an Emmy nomination for his narration of the series.

Speaking of accolades, Brooks is one of only eighteen entertainers to win the EGOT—an acronym for Emmy, Grammy, Oscar, and Tony Awards. In 2009, he received an honor from Kennedy Center Honors. The following year, he was given a Hollywood Walk of Fame star. In 2013, he was honored with the American Film Institute Life Achievement Award; in 2015, he was given a British Film Institute Fellowship. The following year he received a National Medal of Arts; in 2017, a BAFTA Fellowship from the British Academy of Film and Television Arts; and in 2023, an Honorary Academy Award.

After all of his success, however, when most people think of Mel Brooks, they still think of *Blazing Saddles* and *Young Frankenstein*. When I mentioned to Steve Haberman that I couldn't think of many filmmakers who had the one-two punch in the same year as Brooks had with *Blazing Saddles* and *Young Frankenstein*, he quickly pointed out,

> Hitchcock made *Rebecca* and *Foreign Correspondent* in the same year, and they were both nominated for Best Picture. It was easier to do when movies were made in industrial conditions. They're not made that way anymore. Every movie that gets made now is like opening a deli. You have to have a lot of agreement from investors and studios and stars and this and that in order to make a movie now.
>
> In the old days, the studios had a quota of movies they had to make for the theaters and so a guy like John Ford would

go from making *Stagecoach* to *Young Mr. Lincoln* to *Long Voyage Home* to *The Grapes of Wrath* to *How Green Was My Valley* all in a row! How about Hitchcock? He made *Vertigo*, *North by Northwest*, *Psycho*, *The Birds*, and *Marnie*—in a row! We'll never see that again. That will never happen again. We don't have factories that manufacture movies anymore. So you're not going to have any artist who's going to be able to emerge quickly and potently and build on their own vision year after year, movie after movie, because those guys worked in movies like it was their job; it was a nine-to-five job. Monday through Friday, you made movies. That doesn't happen anymore. In the 1970s, it was a rare occurrence; however, as I recall, Coppola made *The Godfather Part II* and *The Conversation* to come out in the same year. That's not bad!

But Mel was on a run there. He was not given the respect that he was due before *Blazing Saddles*, because *The Producers*—although it won the Oscar for Best Screenplay—didn't do well. It didn't make a lot of money. It became a cult film, but that's not the same as being a hit, especially in the business. And *The Twelve Chairs* was also not a hit. There was a four-year hiatus between *The Twelve Chairs* and *Blazing Saddles*.

Haberman also pointed out that, during that hiatus, agent David Begelman—who later in the seventies took over Columbia Pictures and was involved in a studio embezzlement scandal and ended up committing suicide—came to Brooks to help him out.

Mel told me this story, and I'm not sure I believe it; Mel was just walking down the street and Begelman came up to him and said, "Hey, Mel, looking for change?" That's what Mel told me he said to him. And Begelman said, "Listen, I've got a movie for you. I've got a script for you." And he gave him *Black Bart*. And Mel read it, and he saw something in it, and he said, "Yeah, I'll do it if I can pick a gang of writers and rewrite this thing." And Begelman said, "Go for it."

And Mel was out of the business, pretty much, but he had a few friends.

Haberman also noted that the fact that Brooks was married to Anne Bancroft, who was doing very well at the time, didn't hurt during those somewhat lean years, and that kept him in mainstream circles, at least around the edges. "But you're right," Haberman told me, "with the one-two punch of *Blazing Saddles* and *Young Frankenstein*, he was hot."

When I asked Haberman what he thinks the ultimate secret to the success of Mel Brooks has been over the years, he gave me a one-word answer: "Pineapple!"

This required an explanation, I informed him, and he continued: "That's Mel's answer. When people ask him, what's the secret to your longevity, he says, 'Pineapple! Ya gotta eat a lotta pineapple! You get a nice pineapple, you cut it up, you eat that.'"

Haberman has his own idea about why Brooks is so successful: "It's because he's funny! If you make a horror movie and it's scary, you will be successful. If you make a comedy and it's funny, you will be successful. If you make a western and it's exciting, you will be successful. If you set out to do what you want to do, and especially if you do it at a high level, you will be successful. And that's it. Mel is funny, and some say he's the funniest man alive."

And while that may be true, I'll leave the final word to Brooks himself:

"Pineapple!"

Bibliography

Arnold, Gary. "*Blazing Saddles* on a Dead Horse." *Washington Post*, March 7, 1974.

Barnes, Clive. "Not Quite a Monster." *New York Post*, November 9, 2007.

Brooks, Mel. *Young Frankenstein: The Story of the Making of the Film*. New York: Black Dog & Leventhal, 2016.

Brooks, Mel. *All About Me*. New York: Ballantine Books, 2021.

Canby, Vincent. "Screen: *Blazing Saddles* a Western in Burlesque." *New York Times*, February 8, 1974.

Champlin, Charles. "Was the West Ever Like This?" *Los Angeles Times*, February 7, 1974.

Dawson, Jan. "*Blazing Saddles*." *The Monthly Film Bulletin*, June 1974.

Ebert, Roger. "*Blazing Saddles*." *Chicago Sun-Times*, February 7, 1974.

Hallenbeck, Bruce G. *Comedy-Horror Films: A Chronological History, 1914–2008*. Jefferson, NC: McFarland, 2008.

Hirschfeld, Gerald. "The Story of the Filming of *Young Frankenstein*." *American Cinematographer*, July 1974.

Siskel, Gene. "Shootout at 'Cockeyed Corral.'" *Chicago Tribune*, March 1, 1974.

Spencer, Charles. "*Young Frankenstein:* Struggling to Come Back to
    Life." *Daily Telegraph*, November 9, 2007.

Staff writers. "*Blazing Saddles*," *Variety*, February 13, 1974.

Wilder, Gene. *Kiss Me Like a Stranger: My Search for Love and Art*. New
    York: St. Martin's Griffin, 2006.

Index